Poststructural Policy Analysis

Carol Bacchi • Susan Goodwin

Poststructural Policy Analysis

A Guide to Practice

palgrave
macmillan

Carol Bacchi
Department of Politics
University of Adelaide
Adelaide, Australia

Susan Goodwin
Faculty of Education and Social Work
University of Sydney
Sydney, New South Wales, Australia

ISBN 978-1-137-52544-4 ISBN 978-1-137-52546-8 (eBook)
DOI 10.1057/978-1-137-52546-8

Library of Congress Control Number: 2016949395

Cover illustration: Pattern adapted from an Indian cotton print produced in the 19th century

Printed on acid-free paper

This Palgrave Pivot imprint is published by Springer Nature
The registered company is Nature America Inc.
The registered company address is: 1 New York Plaza, New York, NY 10004, U.S.A.

Acknowledgments

We would like to thank Anne Wilson for her excellent advice and expert assistance in the development and preparation of this book. Her attention to detail and engagement with the material have added enormously to the clarity of the ideas presented. We also gratefully acknowledge Jennifer Bonham's contribution to the book and her work with Carol developing a new framework for undertaking poststructural interview analysis. This addition to the book contributes substantially to the objective of providing new and exciting ways to engage questions about policy and governing practices.

Contents

PART I

Asking New Policy Questions

CHAPTER 1

Introduction

Abstract The Introduction articulates how a poststructural approach to policy analysis provides an important vehicle for questioning how governing takes place. It begins by sketching the broad parameters of a poststructural approach as a form of critical analysis that allows a refreshing skepticism toward the full range of things commonly associated with policy: policy itself, the knowledges that support policy and policy proposals, as well as conventional forms of policy analysis. The implication of this form of critical analysis for policy work is explained—how a poststructural approach encourages policy workers to reflect on their own role in governing and to engage in the productive and political practices of interrogating, theorizing, and resisting. The Introduction also sets out the structure of the book.

Keywords poststructuralism · policy analysis · policy work · Foucault · government · governmentality · policy anthropology · policy sociology · WPR approach

This book targets a wide audience—all those influenced by the ways in which governing takes place; in other words, everyone! More specifically, it is directed to those involved in policy development, policy-making, and policy analysis, and those studying these topics. The poststructural perspective it offers encourages policy workers and policy analysts to ask novel and challenging questions about the roles they play in policy development

C. Bacchi, S. Goodwin, *Poststructural Policy Analysis*,
DOI 10.1057/978-1-137-52546-8_1

and how they do their work. In this Introduction, the emphasis is on what a poststructural approach can bring to policy analysis. How is policy thought about differently through a poststructural lens? What is gained from a poststructural perspective in the policy domain?

Poststructuralism is not a singular theory. Still it is possible to identify some broad parameters of a poststructural approach. There is, in general, a questioning of Enlightenment assumptions concerning reason, emancipation, science and progress, and disquiet regarding connections between this thinking and social inequality. Attention is directed to the heterogeneous practices, in particular the knowledge practices, that produce hierarchical and inegalitarian forms of rule. By emphasizing a plurality of practices, it becomes possible to insist that the realities we live are contingent, open to challenge and change. Because things could be otherwise, the firming up of particular social arrangements is seen to involve politics, used here in an expansive sense to mean the active shaping or making of the taken for granted.

The emphasis on heterogeneity and contingency offers a refreshing skepticism about the full range of "things" usually associated with policy, including policy itself. Rather than essences, "things" are "done" or "made", constituted, or brought into being. It follows that "things" commonly treated as entities (e.g., "organizations", "institutions", "the economy", "nation-states"), can also be "undone" or "unmade". Similarly, political "subjects" are understood to be emergent or in process, shaped in ongoing interactions with discourses and other practices, rather than founding or unchanging types of being who possess a fixed human essence or nature. Numerous concepts prove useful in making these arguments, though these can be drawn upon selectively: discourse, subjectification, practices, power-knowledge, governmentality, enactment, performativity, social construction, contestation, reflexivity, among others. Key concepts are introduced in Chapter 3.

While poststructuralism has been extremely influential across the humanities and social sciences, in the field of policy research and analysis it occupies a less well-articulated and more contested position. This gap, we suggest, needs to be addressed. This book aims to provide a succinct and accessible overview of what it means to analyze policy from a Foucault-influenced poststructural perspective, as elaborated in subsequent chapters. It presents a case for why it is important to undertake this form of critical analysis by showing the value of rethinking policy development through a poststructural lens.

A starting point for these reflections is that, as Wendy Brown (1998) suggests, we live in societies "saturated" with policy. From the moment we get up in the morning until we go bed—and even in bed—a panoply of legislative rules and regulations shape what we do and influence how we act. Going further, a poststructural perspective highlights how these rules and regulations bring into play a wide range of professional and "expert" knowledges that have a significant role in how we are governed and in producing the kinds of "subject" we are encouraged to become.

This use of knowledges in the plural signals the skepticism mentioned above—the premises and proposals associated with disciplines, including political science, psychology, epidemiology, social work, anthropology, and so on, are seen as *contingent* historical creations, human constructions, that need to be interrogated rather than enshrined as "truth". This kind of approach can be unsettling. Seeing knowledges as constructed or "made" can dislodge some of the certainties and orthodoxies upon which conventional policy approaches are based. Consider, for example, Sophie Watson's (2000: 73) interrogation of her own discipline, social policy: "in Foucauldian terms social policy is a highly normative discipline which constructs ideal models of society based on notions of social justice which disguise the concrete functioning of power". Yet it is precisely this perspective that enables her to begin to see the complex and contradictory effects apparently benign policies may have. The skepticism poststructuralism brings to knowledges and other "things" is signaled through the use of what are called scare quotes, such as we have inserted. Indeed, wherever we fear that the contingency of a term is not immediately visible we will place it in quotation marks to make it so, e.g., "subjects", "objects", "places", and "problems".[1]

In a poststructural understanding, government involves more than conventional legislative institutions and political parties. It is broader even than civil society and social movements. It includes numerous sites, agencies, and "ways of knowing" that interrelate in important ways to shape social rules. Foucault proposed the term *government* be defined, in general, to mean the "conduct of conduct" (Gordon 1991: 2). In this broader understanding, government refers to any form of activity that aims to shape, guide, or affect the conduct of people. Government can concern how people monitor or regulate their own conduct, how interpersonal relations are guided and controlled, as well as the state-generated rules, regulations, provisions, and punishments we usually associate with the term. "Policy" in this view refers to how order is maintained through politics, understood as the heterogeneous strategic relations that shape lives and worlds.

An important part of this "order maintaining" activity involves categorization: of "objects" (e.g., "traffic", "addiction", "literacy"); of "subjects" (e.g., "citizens", "low SES", "asylum seekers"); and "places" (e.g., "the state", "Europe"). Looking specifically at "subjects", Shore and Wright (2003: 4) make the important point that "from the cradle to the grave, people are classified, shaped and ordered according to policies". Thinking about such categories as the effects of policies rather than as necessary and natural ways of grouping people creates an opening to consider how they are produced and how they translate into diverse lived realities. Annemarie Mol (1999) introduces the concept of ontological politics to emphasize that such lived realities are created by, rather than reflected in, social practices, including policy and research practices.

With this broader canvas, policy workers are encouraged to reflect on the role they play in governing practices. How do the specific tasks they undertake contribute to shaping social order? What assumptions about people and the world underpin their activities and the policies to which they contribute? What sorts of effects follow from governing in a particular way, effects that are typically ignored in a focus on "measurable outcomes"?

These are some of the questions pursued in the book. To assist in this project we introduce a simple tool called "What's the Problem Represented to be?" or the WPR approach to policy analysis. As is outlined in Chapter 2, this "how to" guide or "analytic strategy" brings together a sequence of questions that allows an opening up of policies to the kind of interrogation signaled above. An explicit challenge to the conventional view that policies *address* problems, it approaches policies as problematizations that *produce* "problems" as particular types of problems. By asking how "problems" are represented or constituted in policies, it becomes possible to probe underlying assumptions that render these representations intelligible and the implications that follow for how lives are imagined and lived.

Earlier we claimed that poststructuralism has occupied a less well-articulated and more contested position in the field of policy analysis than in some other areas of social research and practice. But there *are* well-developed pockets of policy research in the social sciences that have been shaped by, and have shaped, poststructural thinking. In the past 40 years, subfields or subdisciplines have emerged out of engagements with poststructuralism: "policy anthropology" is one, "policy sociology" another, as well as the field of "governmentality studies" that traverses many of the social and political sciences (including policy anthropology and policy sociology). These contributions and insights have shaped our own thinking about policy and policy analysis and have, in some cases, quite clearly contributed to the thinking of policy analysts who have deployed the analytic strategy which is the focus of this book: the "What's the Problem Represented to be?" (WPR) approach.

Anthropologists influenced by Foucault, for example, have opened up new perspectives on the study of policy through a focus on policy as a cultural phenomenon. By seeing policy as cultural, it is possible to reflect on the way policy has become an increasingly central concept and instrument in the organization of contemporary societies. Similar to the concepts "family", "society", or "nation", "policy" is a key way of conceptualizing and symbolizing social relations. As Shore and Wright (2011: 2) argue: "There are few, if any, populations today that are not in some way or another touched by the classificatory logics and regulatory powers of policy". Shore (2012: 90; emphasis in original) distinguishes the anthropological approach from conventional policy analysis in this way:

> Whereas most scholars tend to treat policy as a given, seldom questioning its meaning or ontological status as a category, an anthropology *of* policy starts from the premise that "policy" is itself a curious and problematic social and cultural construct that needs to be unpacked and contextualized if its meanings are to be understood.

In making this distinction, Shore invokes the kind of skepticism introduced above: policies are contingent historical creations, human constructions, that produce effects.

The usual approach within policy scholarship, however, is to treat policy as axiomatic or self-evident: society must be ordered, and policy is a practical, natural, or sensible way of doing so. This positivist tendency to treat policies as objective entities—the results of decisions made by rational authorities, ostensibly to address known problems to produce desired outcomes—is one of the reasons policy anthropologists contend that "policy analysis needs to be rescued from policy analysts" (Shore 2012: 92). For example, Shore and Wright (2011: 8) suggest that given the capacity of trained anthropologists "to understand the meanings and subjective understandings of policy makers and, at the same time, to challenge received wisdom and think outside of the conventional policy box", they have an "analytic edge" over policy analysts who have difficulty stepping outside the conceptual schema of "policy science". Yet poststructuralism challenges the privileging of all forms of expertise and knowledge and, as such, the implication that policy analysts are mere technicians who are produced by and who produce policy. In poststructuralism, both theorists and practitioners are treated as "subjects" in process, and as immersed in taken-for-granted knowledges that require critical scrutiny. Chapter 2 elaborates how the questions in a WPR analytic strategy facilitate this practice of self-problematization.

Poststructural ideas have also influenced sociologists to reflect on taken-for-granted notions of policy in particular social fields, particularly education policy, health policy, and social policy. Stephen Ball (1990; 1993; 2015), a proponent of policy sociology, draws on Foucault's theory of discourse to describe policy as discourse. Describing policy *as* discourse directs attention to "the way in which policy ensembles, or collections of related policies, exercise power through a *production* of 'truth' and 'knowledge'" (Ball 1993: 14; emphasis in original). Following Foucault, Ball's characterization of policy as discourse emphasizes the constitutive, or productive, nature of policies. In this approach, rather than focusing on how people make policy, attention turns to the way policy makes people. At the same time, Ball attends to the "creative social activity" (1993: 12) and "agency" (2015: 307) of those (such as teachers) who, in his terms, *enact* policy, challenging the commonly assumed separation between policy generation and policy implementation.

Sociologists (Coffee 2004; Lall 2012) have been increasingly drawn into the research task of identifying "dominant discourses" in educational, health, and social policy, and there has been a great deal of attention given to the operation of the contemporary "discourses" of neoliberalism and management theory in these areas. When these "discourses" are conceptualized as monolithic and determining, there is a tendency to envisage policy work as necessarily implicated in the rolling out of neoliberalism and/or managerialism. To protect against this tendency, Ball (1997: 261) highlights the existence of "pockets of resilience and counter-discursive activity". The applications of WPR in this book illustrate precisely this form of activity.

Governmentality scholars working with Foucault have provided the most visible questioning of "policy", and their arguments are looked at more closely in Chapter 3 and elsewhere in the book. Put briefly, governmentality refers to the way of thinking—or mentality—that allows the exercise of power by social authorities to manage populations in modern polities (Miller and Rose 1990: 2). Governmentality scholars are interested in what makes modern government possible, including how the governmental schemes and programs put in place make sense to those who govern, as well as to those who are governed. They have focused attention on (at least) three key themes that make up this "will to govern": political rationalities (ways of thinking about what governing entails); the technologies or techniques involved in governing; and the "subjects" of government, or the diverse forms of persons that are presupposed and also delivered by governmental activity.

The focus in governmentality literature on the "programmatic character of government", described as an "eternal optimism" about developing programs to administer society better (Miller and Rose 1990: 4), is often accompanied by references to policy makers and policy workers as "programmers" and administrators (Miller and Rose 1990: 4, 27–28; Rose et al. 2006: 86, 99). However, as O'Malley et al. (1997: 513) note, there is space within a governmentality perspective to recognize a "constitutive role for contestation (among rulers, and between and among those who are ruled)". In line with this perspective, we wish to avoid "fixing" the role, identity, or work of the policy analyst as a technician or a programmer, to see, instead, the policy worker *cum* analyst as engaged in the practices of interrogating, criticizing, and evaluating policies, and through these practices, unmaking and re-making policy. Indeed, we see it as our task to provide a tool to facilitate exactly this form of critique. To this end, in Chapter 2, we offer the WPR approach as an analytic strategy to facilitate these practices, and hence to promote a poststructural sensibility. Such an approach, we suggest, enables policy workers to reflect critically on governing practices, to theorize their location within those practices, and to resist practices deemed to have deleterious consequences for specific people and groups.

This characterization of policy work and policy workers, we acknowledge, does not fit with the modernist conception of the policy worker deploying scientific methods in the service of solving social problems, gathering "evidence", creating social order, or contributing to societal "progress". But our project is to disrupt these certainties. From a Foucault-influenced poststructural perspective, policy work, like all knowledge work, is political work; policy research, like all research, is understood as a form of ontological politics (Mol 1999) that makes worlds.

Remaking policy analysis as political work is especially timely given the reaffirmation of rationalist approaches in contemporary policy worlds. In contrast to the developments we have described here, the "evidence-based policy movement" is positioning the policy analyst as an expert trained in specific analytical techniques which they apply systematically to inform policy production (Shaw 2010). This "new face" of policy analysis involves conceiving policy in a very traditional way—as rational, orderly, and capable of producing objective solutions to problems. Once again, knowledge is seen as uncontested, capable of being translated into policy under the rubric of "what works".

At the same time, we believe the space for revisiting fixed ideas about the identity of the policy worker has well and truly opened up: many text books outlining theories and concepts in public policy, educational policy, social policy, even economic policy, now introduce poststructural perspectives, even if only briefly. For example, *Analyzing Public Policy* (1998) describes public policy as traditionally embodying theories of knowledge that have "their origins in scientific epistemology" (John 1998: 164) and suggests that work using Foucault challenges this position. From this alternative perspective, policy "cannot be seen as the expression of a neutral rationality, but it is the expression of knowledge as power" (John 1998: 165). In *An Introduction to Australian Public Policy: Theory and Practice* (Maddison and Denniss 2013), readers are introduced to the poststructural idea that policy work is a "problematizing activity" and to Bacchi's (2009) perspective that governing takes place through problematizations. In the British social policy text *Understanding Theories and Concepts in Social Policy* (Lister 2010), a full chapter is dedicated to policies as social constructions that constitute "problems". These books encourage the production of policy workers who think about policy, even if only partially or fleetingly, through a poststructural lens that queries the categories and concepts with which they work on a day-to-day basis.

In a similar way, policy guides and handbooks for policy workers alert readers to the possibilities poststructural approaches lend to the activities of policy work, although these possibilities are often lined up alongside modernist approaches, as though they are but one option among many (Sutton 1999; Lall 2007). In addition, feminist contributions to policy analysis, for example, Bina Fernandez (2012), in *Transformative Policy for Poor Women* and Elizabeth Allan (2012), in *Policy Discourses, Gender, and Education*, have developed strategies, in the form of frameworks, for *doing* poststructural policy analysis. The concomitance between feminist policy analysts "fond of poststructural critiques" (St. Pierre 2000: 477) and Foucault-influenced poststructuralism is particularly striking. Certain

Foucauldian concepts have proved useful in, for example, challenging the separation between "public" politics and "private" activities, questioning policy categories that tend to install essentialist identities, and expanding policy analysis to include critical interrogation of the activities and knowledges of experts, professionals, and researchers, illustrated in subsequent chapters. These examples indicate that space has opened up for the kind of poststructural interrogation and contestation of policy we introduce here.

Most importantly, some policy workers/analysts are already engaged in deploying the specific analytic strategy at the center of this book, the WPR approach. Applications of the WPR approach include examples from Australia, the UK, Germany, Canada, Sweden and other Scandinavian countries, and from New Zealand and India. They explore a range of policy areas, including health policy, welfare policy, immigration policy, family policy, equity policy, education policy, drug and alcohol policy, development policy, and economic policy. The authors (and readers) of these WPR applications cannot be considered to be *outside* of policy work, evaluating policy on terms from elsewhere. Nor, borrowing Feldman's (2007 in Shore 2012: 89) useful phrase, can they be seen as simply following "the policy gaze". They are *inside* the work of policy, conducting deep critical evaluations of what is constituted, or made, by policy, and how this process of making occurs. For this reason, we reconstruct the category of policy analysts to include policy workers and policy makers, indicated in the conventions "policy workers/analysts" and "policy workers *cum* analysts".

It is, indeed, *because* a corpus of policy work in the WPR "tradition" now exists that we can take the time ourselves to read, interpret, and evaluate what is being made using the WPR approach and provide an account of what this Foucault-influenced poststructural analytic strategy can do. The remainder of Part I introduces the WPR analytic strategy (Chapter 2) and elaborates the key theoretical concepts upon which it relies (Chapter 3). In Part II of the book, we marshal the outcomes of various WPR projects (in a range of countries and in a range of fields) under key themes: making and unmaking "problems"; making and unmaking "subjects"; making and unmaking "objects"; and making and unmaking "places". Organizing our assessment in this way is heuristic: a helpful procedure for revealing what the WPR approach can do, rather than a proof of the method. In laying this work out in this way, the account is relevant to policy analysts across policy domains and policy settings.

Note

1. The use of scare quotes to signal contingency is particularly important for the treatment of "problems", since the book is concerned to put in question the common assumption in many approaches to policy analysis that "problems" simply exist and that their meaning is clear and uncontentious (see Chapter 4). Scare quotes will be omitted only in those cases where it is evident that a specific theoretical stance approaches objects, subjects, places, and problems as unproblematized "entities".

CHAPTER 2

Making Politics Visible: The WPR Approach

Abstract This chapter offers an analytic strategy, or "tool", called "What's the Problem Represented to be?" (the WPR approach), to facilitate poststructural policy analysis. It elaborates a poststructural understanding of politics as strategic relations and practices, and of theorizing as political practice. The WPR approach is introduced as a means to engage in such theorizing and to assist in the analytic task of making politics visible. To this end it offers seven interrelated forms of questioning and analysis to critically scrutinize problematizations (the ways in which "problems" are produced and represented) in governmental policies and practices, understood in broad terms. Policy workers and other analysts are enjoined to deploy WPR in practices of interrogating problematizations, reproblematization, and self-problematization.

Keywords politics · essentialism · becoming · contestation · critique · silences · "the real" · problem representation · WPR approach

In the Introduction, we positioned policy workers as involved in theorizing. Here we proceed to introduce the "tool", referred to as the WPR approach, that we offer to facilitate this critical practice. Because the "What's the Problem Represented to be?" (WPR) approach offers a way of thinking differently about commonly accepted categories and governing practices, it is relevant also to students and scholars in many other

C. Bacchi, S. Goodwin, *Poststructural Policy Analysis*,
DOI 10.1057/978-1-137-52546-8_2

fields, including sociology, social work, anthropology, cultural studies, and human geography.

WPR is an analytic strategy that puts in question the common view that the role of governments is to solve problems that sit outside them, waiting to be "addressed". Rather, it considers how governmental practices, understood broadly, produce "problems" as particular kinds of problems. Alongside and through the production of "problems", governmental practices contribute to the production of "subjects", "objects", and "places" (see Part II). The WPR approach heralds the importance of directing critical attention to this *productive* activity. What exactly is produced? How is it produced? And, with what effects?

An underlying goal is to make the politics involved in these productive practices visible. Countering the commonly touted view that "objects" are clearly "objects", people are just "humans", and countries and other geographical entities simply *exist*, attention shifts to considering how these "things" have come to be and continue to be "done" or "made" on an ongoing basis. Since "things" are not "natural", since they are made to be, they involve politics. This expansive understanding of politics extends well beyond political institutions, parties, and so on to include the *heterogeneous strategic relations and practices* that shape who we are and how we live.

From a poststructural perspective, phenomena are not singular, fixed, or discrete entities that can be attributed an essence. Instead, they are best viewed as combinations or patterned networks of diverse elements and relations that are coordinated, arranged, combined, or patterned to *appear* as a convergence. This heterogeneous arrangement is regarded as "strategic" in accordance with Foucault's argument that such arrangements involve "strategies without strategists". "The mechanisms brought into play in power relations are 'strategic' but are not the property or achievement of autonomous agents" (Ezzamel and Willmott 2010: 90).

There is no suggestion of conspiracy; nor is there talk of "vested interests". Rather, Foucault (1979: 26) refers to a "micro-physics of power", to ensure recognition of the plural and diverse practices involved in the production of "things".

Sawicki (1991) captures these distinctive contours of a Foucault-influenced approach, as it would be applied to policies surrounding new reproductive technologies in the US:

> Thinking specifically about the history of childbirth in America, a Foucauldian feminist does not assume a priori that the new reproductive

> technologies are the product of a long-standing male "desire" to control women's bodies or to usurp procreation.... Employing a bottom-up analysis, a Foucauldian feminist would describe the present situation as the outcome of a myriad of micro-practices, struggles, tactics and counter-tactics. (Sawicki 1991: 80–81)

In addition, assumptions about the *being* of "things" are replaced by references to their *becoming* (Chia 1996). The physicality of "objects" is not questioned. However, "objects" are seen as in continuous development, as "in formation", rather than as fixed. In effect, practices and relations *replace* "objects" (Veyne 1997). Hence, "things" become open-ended and malleable, creating space for contestation and *unmaking*. "Subjects" too are considered to be in a process of continuous development, rejecting an essentialism that portrays human beings as sovereign subjects who grasp meaning intuitively (Foucault 1972: 227).

A particular way of thinking about "knowledge" is at work here. "Knowledge", such as that produced in research, is no longer treated as "truth" or as a set of "true" statements about "reality". Instead, "knowledges" are seen to play a critical role in governing practices and in the making of "reality". In line with this view, the production of "knowledge", through research, is understood to be a form of political practice. The term "ontological politics" captures this proposition that research *makes*, rather than *reflects*, worlds (Mol 2002).

Such a stance challenges policy workers *cum* analysts to reflect critically on the "methods" they use and the categories of analysis they adopt. Foucault offers some pointers as to the form of critique that is required. He states:

> A critique does not consist in saying that things aren't good the way they are. It consists in seeing on what type of assumptions, of familiar notions, of established, unexamined ways of thinking the accepted practices are based. (Foucault 1994a: 456)

Barbara Johnson (1981: xv) elaborates:

> It [a critique] is an analysis that focuses on the grounds of the system's possibility. The critique reads backwards from what seems natural, obvious, self-evident, or universal to show that these things have their history, their reasons for being the way they are, their effects on what follows from them, and that the starting point is not a (natural) given but a (cultural) construct, usually blind to itself.

In effect, here, Foucault and Johnson outline the agenda for a WPR analysis, as illustrated in the accompanying Chart (see WPR Chart on page 20). Its seven interrelated forms of questioning and analysis "work backwards" from policy proposals to *examine* the "unexamined ways of thinking" on which they rely, to put in question their underlying premises, to show that they have a history, and to insist on questioning their implications. The intent, displayed in the question format, is not to reveal "truths", which would contradict its poststructural commitments, but to encourage a particular kind of interrogation, as elaborated below.

The key term in a WPR analytic practice is problematization. The word can be used in two ways, *either* to signal a form of critical analysis, putting something into question, *or* to refer to the products of governmental practices, that is, how issues are problematized (see Chapter 3). Pursuing the latter meaning, Rose and Miller (1992: 181) describe "government" as a "problematizing activity". As Osborne (1997: 174) explains, the suggestion here is that "policy cannot get to work without first problematizing its territory". In other words, to intervene, to institute a policy, "government", including but beyond the state, has to target something as a "problem" that needs fixing.

The dominant view in most approaches to policy is that the task of government is (simply) to address and to attempt to solve "problems that exist". *Problem-solving* is a recurrent mantra. The intent and purpose of the WPR approach is to challenge this premise. It makes the case that policies do not *address* problems that exist; rather, they *produce* "problems" as particular sorts of problems. Further, it is argued that the manner in which these "problems" are constituted shapes lives and worlds. The critical task, therefore, becomes interrogating the particular problematizations within policies. This study of governmental problematizations provides a means to make visible the politics—in the broad sense discussed above—involved in the making of "problems".

The WPR approach starts from a simple idea: that what we propose to do about something indicates what we think needs to change and hence what we think the "problem" is. This thinking can be applied to policies. Because they are proposals for change of some sort, they produce or constitute a particular representation of the "problem" they purport to address. It follows that it is possible to "read off" the implied "problem"—what is seen as in need of "fixing"—from specific policy proposals or plans of action. If, for example, activity regimes for children are introduced as a way to reduce childhood "obesity", the "problem" is constituted as children's inactivity. By contrast, if regulations are introduced to limit the amount of advertising of fast food during prime time children's television, the "problem" of "obesity" is represented to be aggressive or, perhaps, even unethical advertising.

Another way to make this point is to note that childhood "obesity" is *problematized* differently in the two contrasting proposals. Importantly, the concern here is not how different *people* might problematize the issue but how the *policy itself* problematizes it (see Bacchi 2015a). The problematization forms a part of the policy. Moreover, to say that a policy *represents* a "problem" in a particular way does not imply that we are talking about an image or impression of the "problem", as if we could wish it otherwise. Rather, we are talking about how the "problem" is *made to be* a particular kind of problem *within a specific policy*, with all sorts of effects. The subsequent claim is that we are *governed through* these constituted "problems", meaning that governing takes place through problematizations.

Bacchi (2009) coins the term "problem representation" to refer to the form of a problematization or the problematized phenomenon in a specific site. The analytic task becomes teasing out the conceptual premises underpinning problem representations, tracing their genealogy, reflecting on the practices that sustain them and considering their effects (see Chapter 3). Harking back to Johnson (1981: xv; above), the objective is to examine critically the "grounds of the system's possibility", the politics involved in its making.

The simple idea that it is possible to "work backwards" from a proposal to how a "problem" is represented—to "read off" the problem representation from the proposal or proposed solution—can be applied in a vast array of contexts. It promotes a novel way of thinking that opens up many kinds of material to original and inventive interrogation. For example, this thinking can be applied to theoretical or academic analyses, which are in effect forms of proposal. Concepts, too, can be seen as proposals (Tanesini 1994; see Chapter 6). The same kind of thinking can be used to instigate critical analysis of some forms of media material. "Working backwards" from the proposals in such material—theories, academic analyses, concepts, media representations—provides the opportunity to examine and reflect critically on the deep-seated assumptions upon which they are based.

The focus of this book is the application of this way of thinking in the realm of policy. Policy, as explained in the Introduction, is understood in an expansive sense to include both the activities of state institutions and of other agencies and professions involved in maintaining social order. For policy workers *cum* analysts, written texts can provide useful starting points. Thus policy texts can include documents, such as organizational files and records, legislation, judicial decisions, bills, speeches, interview transcripts (see Appendix), media statements, organizational charts, budgets, program contracts, research reports, even statistical data. In particular policy sites, written texts could include institutional records, organizational reports, syllabi, etc. "Texts" can be understood expansively to include images, videos and forms of digital communication (e.g., websites, hyperlinks across websites; see Marshall 2012b).

Importantly, if a text is selected for analysis, it provides only a starting point. The WPR approach does not involve a study of modes of language use or rhetoric. It therefore stands at a distance from the so-called "linguistic turn" where the focus is primarily on the content and linguistic construction of a text (Fairclough 2013). By way of contrast, the WPR approach uses texts as "levers" to open up reflections on the forms of governing, and associated effects, instituted through a particular way of constituting a "problem". To deploy this "lever" necessarily involves familiarity with other texts that cover the same or related topics or circumstances.

Analysis can also be applied to phenomena that are not literally textual and "objects" not found in formal documents, such as ceremonies (as spoken and acted text), organizational culture (as symbols), buildings, and mechanisms of government. For example, Bottrell and Goodwin (2011: 4) describe how modern schools with their "uni-purpose facilities located on enclosed land, fenced and gated" reflect a "hidden curriculum" that problematizes the moral and cognitive training of young people. As an example of a governmental mechanism, Rowse (2009) shows how the current Australian census problematizes Indigenous peoples as part of a population binary, Indigenous and non-Indigenous, inviting analysis of the sort of political claims such a statistical distinction facilitates or blocks.

The key distinguishing characteristic of the material that can be adopted for a WPR analysis is that it is prescriptive—that it can be understood, possibly in a loose sense, as a *form of proposal* and a guide to conduct. Foucault (1986: 12) described his domain of analysis as "texts written for the purpose of offering rules, opinions, and advice on how to behave as one should". As explained in the Introduction, this focus reflects a broad conception of "government" as "the conduct of conduct", incorporating self-governance, interpersonal relations, relations within communities or institutions, as well as "relations concerned with the exercise of political sovereignty" (Gordon 1991: 2-3). As proposals to guide conduct, the material adopted for analysis will—following the simple idea introduced above—necessarily indicate what is targeted for change and hence what the "problem" is represented to be. To repeat the key point, the WPR approach asks us to identify a "proposal" or a "proposed solution" so that we can "read off" the implicit problem representation within it.

Nikolas Rose (2000: 58) uses the language of "answers" and "questions", instead of "proposals" and "problems", to argue something similar. He says:

> If policies, arguments, analyses and prescriptions purport to provide answers, they do so only in relation to a set of questions. Their very status as answers is dependent upon the existence of such questions. If, for example, imprisonment, marketization, community care are seen as answers, to what are they answers? And, in reconstructing the problematizations which accord them intelligibility as answers, these grounds become visible, their limits and presuppositions are opened for investigation in new ways.

In Rose's analysis, imprisonment, marketization, and community care function as prescriptive guides to conduct that problematize behaviors in particular ways. The critical task becomes reconstructing the problematizations that accord these "guides" (e.g., marketization) intelligibility as *answers*. By reconstructing the problematizations, says Rose, it becomes possible to identify "limits and presuppositions" in the "answers" that demand interrogation.

These exact goals—identifying, reconstructing, and interrogating problematizations—are accomplished through the forms of questioning and analysis in a WPR application. The approach, which is outlined in the Chart below, consists of six questions and an undertaking to apply those questions to one's own policy proposals. Since the seven modes of analysis necessarily involve overlap and some repetition, their listing as separate "steps" serves a heuristic function and ought to be treated accordingly. The remainder of this chapter clarifies how to apply the approach by explaining the goal of each "step" and how to put it into practice.

What's the Problem Represented to be? (WPR) approach to policy analysis

Question 1: What's the problem (e.g., of "gender inequality", "drug use/abuse", "economic development", "global warming", "childhood obesity", "irregular migration", etc.) represented to be in a specific policy or policies?
Question 2: What deep-seated presuppositions or assumptions underlie this representation of the "problem" (*problem representation*)?
Question 3: How has this representation of the "problem" come about?
Question 4: What is left unproblematic in this problem representation? Where are the silences? Can the "problem" be conceptualized differently?
Question 5: What effects (discursive, subjectification, lived) are produced by this representation of the "problem"?
Question 6: How and where has this representation of the "problem" been produced, disseminated and defended? How has it been and/or how can it be disrupted and replaced?
Step 7: Apply this list of questions to your own problem representations.
Adapted from Bacchi, C. (2009), *Analysing Policy: What's the Problem Represented to be?* Pearson Education, Frenchs Forest.

The goal in Question 1 is to identify a place to begin the analysis. We are looking for a way to open up for questioning something that appears natural and obvious (see Johnson 1981 above)—e.g., a specific policy or a governing technique. The selection of a starting point depends upon the pertinence to one's work and political priorities.

In a WPR approach this first step involves identifying a problem representation (see above). To identify a problem representation one "works backwards" from a proposal, broadly understood, to see what is problematized. For example, the governing mechanism of a census (see Rowse 2009) assumes as problematic the shape, number, etc., of a population, which becomes the problem representation. Problem representations provide the springboard, or lever, to the rest of the analysis. It is important to remember that policy texts are often complex constructions that may well involve more than one problem representation.

In this form of analysis, the objective is not to try to identify the intentions behind a particular policy or program. Nor is the goal to assess the distance between promised changes and the failure to deliver those changes—we are not contrasting stated "solutions" with stated "problems", and finding the "solutions" wanting. Rather, we start *from* stated "solutions" to inquire into their *implicit* problematization(s).

Rowse's (2009) example of a census and Rose's (2000) example of marketization indicate that identifying a "proposal" has to be understood in the context of "guides to conduct". One does not need to find an explicit statement or recommendation about "how to behave as one should" (Foucault 1986: 12; see above), though oftentimes such statements do appear in policy directives. More commonly, however, a government report may refer simply to the desirability of some condition such as "social cohesion", signaling thereby that *lack of* social cohesion is represented or constituted to be a problem of sorts. In this way such assertions provide a problem representation, a starting point for interrogation.

The goals in Question 2 are several. First, we consider how this particular problem representation was possible by identifying the meanings (presuppositions, assumptions, "unexamined ways of thinking", knowledges/discourses) that needed to be in place for it to make sense or be intelligible (see Chapter 3). Note that we are seeking these meanings *within* the policy, program or technical instrument, *not* in the heads of social actors (e.g., policy workers, social workers, academics). Second, we identify how the problem representation is constructed—which concepts and binaries, such as public/private, man/woman and citizen/migrant, does it rely upon? Finally, we identify and reflect upon possible patterns in problematizations that might signal the operation of a particular political or governmental rationality (see "Governmentality: Rationalities and Technologies" in Chapter 3).

As indicated above in the reference to knowledges/discourses, in a Foucault-influenced poststructural analysis, discourses refer to knowledges rather than to language. They comprise both general background knowledge, apparent in epistemological and ontological assumptions, and forms of relatively bounded social knowledges, such as disciplines. These knowledges are understood as "in the true" or "sayable" (Foucault 1991a: 58), as forms of truth, rather than as "truth". The task, which Foucault describes as "archaeology", is to critically interrogate these "unexamined ways of thinking" (Foucault 1994a: 456; see above), reflecting on their possible implications. For example, for the census we would consider epidemiology, medicine, social anthropology, etc. For activity regimes to combat childhood "obesity", exercise physiology, occupational science and childhood psychology would all figure as relevant knowledges to examine and question.

To understand how these knowledges acquire "truth" status it is necessary to locate them within the relevant networks of relations and practices that produce them, which Foucault called "discursive practices" (Bacchi and Bonham 2014). These comprise a wide array of elements, including sites, "objects", and subject positions, together with interconnecting mechanisms and processes (see Chapter 3). Relevant to our examples of the census and childhood "obesity" would be the discursive practices of health, biology and security, among others.

The goal in Question 3 of a WPR analysis is to examine how a specific problem representation has come to be. It is important to note that the intent of this question is to challenge any search for origins or any suggestion of some easily traceable evolution of a policy. Rather, the objective is to bring to light the plethora of possible alternative developments. The intent is to disrupt any assumption that what *is* reflects what *has to be.*

Question 3 involves a form of Foucauldian genealogy. It requires the detailed mapping of practices that produce identified problem representations. Differential power relations form an important part of this analysis, considering for example the operation of specific discursive practices that create forms of authority for certain knowledges (see Chapter 3). Particular attention is directed to "subjugated knowledges", those minor knowledges that challenge the scientific consensus and that survive at the margins (Foucault 1980: 83; see Chapter 3).

The goal in Question 4 is to encourage a critical practice of thinking otherwise. The point is to destabilize an existing problem representation by drawing attention to silences, or unproblematized elements, within it. Question 4 also opens up the opportunity to be inventive, to imagine worlds in which a specific confluence of circumstances is either not problematized or problematized differently.

The analyses performed in Questions 2 and 3 prepare the ground for asking Question 4: "What is left unproblematic in this problem representation? Where are the silences? Can the 'problem' be conceptualized differently?" Comparing problematizations of selected issues, across time and cross-culturally, provides a particularly powerful intervention to promote an ability to "think otherwise". Such comparisons help to identify the particular combination of practices and relations that give a "problem" a certain shape in a specific context, and indicate that different practices can produce contrasting problematizations.

Question 5 invites analysts to consider the effects of identified problem representations. Effects ought to be thought about as political implications rather than as measurable "outcomes". Three specific "kinds" of effects are considered—discursive effects, subjectification effects, and lived effects—though these need to be understood as interconnected.

Building on Question 4, a study of *discursive effects* shows how the terms of reference established by a particular problem representation set limits on what can be thought and said. *Subjectification effects* draw attention to how "subjects" are implicated in problem representations, how they are produced as specific kinds of subjects (see Chapter 3). *Lived effects*, as an analytic category, ensures that the ways in which discursive and subjectification effects translate into people's lives form part of the analysis. These interconnected effects can coalesce in what Foucault (1982: 208) calls "dividing practices", which function to separate groups of people from one another and which can also produce "governable subjects" divided within themselves. Taken together, discursive, subjectification, and lived effects bridge a symbolic-material division, showing that the form of analysis promoted here does not reside in some representational universe cut off from daily life. Question 5 thus makes it possible to reflect on the complex array of implications that problematizations entail in certain contexts and to promote interventions that aim to reduce deleterious consequences for specific groups of people.

The earlier questions in the approach lay the groundwork for Question 5. To direct attention to subjectification effects, we return to the discourses identified in Question 2 and focus on the subject positions within them. To investigate the "playing out" of problem representations in people's lives ("lived effects"), it is possible to adopt a wide gamut of empirical techniques, as part of a commitment to selected political goals. Hence, one can include quantitative measures of social location, ethnographic studies of social interactions, interviews, etc., in one's analysis, though the use of this material needs to reflect poststructural premises. For example, such use ought to exclude assumptions about a foundational subject (see Appendix). Also, to be consistent with a poststructural sensibility, judgments on the basis of this material have to remain open to disputation, variation, and revision.

As with Question 3, the purpose of Question 6 is to emphasize the existence and possibility of contestation, to destabilize taken-for-granted "truths". On one side it highlights the practices that install and authorize a particular problem representation. Mol (2002: vii-viii) describes such practices as acts of "coordination" that produce "the real", highlighting the importance of questioning them. On the other side Question 6 opens up space to reflect on forms of resistance and "counter-conduct" (Foucault 1978) that challenge (or could challenge) pervasive and authoritative problem representations (see Chapter 3). Questions 2 and 3 provide material for this part of the analysis.

The last "step" in the WPR approach is an undertaking to apply its six questions to one's *own* proposals and problem representations. The rationale for this commitment to self-problematization is that, given one's location within historically and culturally entrenched forms of knowledge, we need ways to subject our own thinking to critical scrutiny. This theme, commonly described as "reflexivity", is well-rehearsed in contemporary social criticism (Bacchi 2011) but takes on special significance in Foucauldian analysis given Foucault's (2001: 1431) commitment to problematizing "even what we are ourselves" ("*même ce que nous sommes nous-mêmes*"). To this end, the WPR approach moves beyond easy-to-make *declarations* of the need to become "reflexive" to endorse a precise and demanding *activity*—subjecting one's own recommendations and proposals to a WPR analysis.

In terms of practical application of WPR, it is possible to draw selectively upon the forms of questioning and analysis just described, so long as a self-problematizing ethic is maintained. Not every question needs to be asked every time one engages with the critical thinking the approach offers. At the same time, it is highly likely that a WPR analysis may well need to be applied *more than once* in any particular application. This is because problem representations tend to lodge or "nest" one within the other. For example, when Bacchi (2015b) inquired into how the World Health Organization represented the "problem" of alcohol consumption within its reports and associated publications, she found that alcohol use was problematized in terms of "alcohol problems". This "answer" invited the subsequent question—what kinds of "problems" are "alcohol problems" represented to be? This example illustrates the importance of examining the selected body of material carefully for problematizations *within* problematizations.

Questions are sometimes raised about the usefulness of poststructural analysis, in particular Foucault-influenced forms thereof. The suggestion is made that something like WPR leaves us mired in a field of competing interpretations with no precise recommendations on "ways forward".

Foucault (1991b: 84), of course, was explicit in distancing himself from reformers who declared, "this, then, is what needs to be done". And yet, with Foucault, the WPR approach, as seen above, does not shy away from discussions of power and contestation. Indeed, it invites analysis of forms of authority and assessment of effects, and promotes a view of research as political practice.

Is it possible to claim to support an egalitarian politics while refusing to advocate specific reforms? We would argue that, in fact, the two perspectives are not only compatible, they are necessary to each other. This is because reform programs often buy into problematic premises that need highlighting and questioning—as examples, consider the analysis of "social inclusion", "literacy", and "wellbeing" offered in Chapter 6. The goal, therefore, is to create the space to reflect critically on *all* proposals for change, including one's own recommendations, in order to govern "with a minimum of domination" (Foucault 1987: 129). The task, as Foucault (2001: 1431) describes it, is to engage in "a work of problematisation and of perpetual reproblematisation" ("*un travail de problématisation et de perpétuelle reproblématisation*").

In line with this thinking one of the authors (Goodwin) describes four ways in which the WPR approach informed a background paper she wrote on family-centered employment for the Australian Government.

1. I interrogated how and by whom and for what purposes populations were to be governed through this new social program.
2. I had to theorize about the possible harms of different knowledges involved in producing a relationship between families, unemployment, and government for the purposes of social programming.
3. I sought to promulgate an alternative vision in my representation of the relationship between families, unemployment, and government.
4. Participating in this process was political work; it involved engaging in the politics (in the governing) of poverty and family life, and necessitated reflecting on my own views on the policy area.

Goodwin's account provides an example of what WPR brings to the policy table. It illustrates the usefulness of opening up governing practices to critical scrutiny by examining how these practices problematize an issue. It highlights the importance of identifying and assessing the impact of governing knowledges and of promoting less harmful alternatives, while keeping in view one's own problematizations. Most crucially, it indicates the political nature of policy work and invites policy analysts to engage in this politics through the form of theorizing a WPR approach offers. The kinds of new questions promoted by this form of policy analysis include:

- How do specific policies, read broadly, represent the "problems" they claim to address?
- Which knowledge practices are involved in this production of "problems"?
- How do these knowledges acquire authority?
- How do governmental problematizations get played out in people's lives?
- Which scenarios are encouraged? Which alternatives are closed off?
- How are political "subjects" produced within specific problem representations?
- Which "objects" and "places" are created, and with what effects?
- What alternative problematizations are possible?

CHAPTER 3

Key Themes and Concepts

Abstract The "What's the Problem Represented to be?" (WPR) approach invokes a number of concepts that require elaboration. Many rely, at least to an extent, upon the writings of Michel Foucault, indicated in the quotations from his works. This chapter explains how these concepts are interlinked and how they function to produce the form of theorizing enabled by a WPR form of analysis. The following topics are addressed:

- what it means to describe policy as productive;
- the kinds of practices targeted for scrutiny;
- how discourses feature in the analysis;
- what is involved in problematizing and problematization;
- what is achieved by expanding "government" to include the roles of professionals, experts, and allied agencies;
- how genealogy produces a "history of the present";
- the place of political "subjects" in a Foucault-influenced analysis.

Keywords power · practices · discourse · problematization · governmentality · genealogy · subjectification

In order to deploy a "What's the Problem Represented to be?" (WPR) form of analysis, it is necessary to engage with a range of concepts that have long and complicated heritages (e.g., "power", "discourse", and "resistance").

C. Bacchi, S. Goodwin, *Poststructural Policy Analysis*,
DOI 10.1057/978-1-137-52546-8_3

Many of these terms have more than one meaning, depending on the theoretical stance assumed. This chapter elaborates the particular meanings of key concepts adopted in a Foucault-influenced poststructural approach, clarifying distinctions from other intellectual traditions where need be.

Importantly, there is no suggestion that the meanings employed in this text are in some sense "correct". Such a position would directly contradict a poststructural focus on knowledge production, in which concepts play a central role. In this perspective, borrowing from Tanesini (1994: 207), concepts have no fixed meanings but "are proposals about how we ought to proceed from here". This stance follows from Foucault's nominalism, elaborated below, in which the terms we use (e.g., "power", "resistance", etc.) are simply the names that we assign to "things". Hence, the task becomes understanding *particular usages of concepts and their purposes.*

Power, Knowledge, and Resistance

The most common use of the term "power" in everyday speech and in much of policy analysis is to mean "power over", in which some people (those *with* power) dominate other people (who *lack* power). For example, some within an interpretive analytic tradition (see later) describe power as the *possession* of "powerful elites" (Turnbull 2005: 210). By contrast, poststructural accounts, such as the WPR approach, adopt "more systemic, less agent specific, perceptions of power that see it as more generally constitutive of reality" (Haugaard and Clegg 2009: 3). A number of related concepts have been developed to support and explore this constitutive—or productive—understanding of power: "doing", "practices" (discussed in the next section of this chapter), "performativity", "enactment", and "becoming" (as opposed to "being").

Foucault's comments on power assist in understanding the poststructural position. Adopting a nominalist perspective, power is not considered to be a "thing" that is possessed by sovereign subjects standing outside power; rather, it is "the name that one attributes to a complex strategical situation in a particular society" (Foucault 1990a: 93). The language of *power relations*, therefore, replaces references to power *tout court.*

Nor is power a normative category; "relations of power are not something bad in themselves, from which one must free one's self" (Foucault 1987: 129). Yet there are various types of power relationships—ranging from fluid, shifting relationships between individuals, to situations where power relations "congeal" in "states of domination" (Foucault 1987: 114).

Between these extremes are forms of power that Foucault describes as "techniques of government", which are established systems for regulating the conduct of conduct (see "Governmentality: Rationalities and Technologies"). These techniques require analysis "because it is often through this kind of technique that states of domination are established and maintain themselves" (Foucault 1987: 130). Within this complex relationship among forms of power, the objective, says Foucault, is "to give one's self the rules of law, the techniques of management, and also the ethics, the *ethos*, the practices of self, which would allow these games of power to be played with a minimum of domination" (Foucault 1987: 130).

Power relations, moreover, are not solely to do with prohibition and repression. Rather, they "have a directly productive role, wherever they come into play" (Foucault 1990a: 94). In this view, power relations make "things" come into existence:

> We must cease once and for all to describe the effects of power in negative terms: it "excludes," it "represses," it "censors," it "abstracts," it "masks," it "conceals." In fact, power produces; it produces reality; it produces domains of objects and rituals of truth. The individual and the knowledge that may be gained of him (sic) belong to this production. (Foucault 1984a: 204–205)

The critical task, therefore, becomes tracing and assessing the *specific forms* of reality that power creates. For example, Foucault draws attention to governmental regulation of biological processes of the population, which he calls "biopower". Such regulation, he argues, *produces* docile and productive bodies, and a healthy and vigorous social body (Foucault 1990a: 141).

Foucault's understanding of power as relational and productive underpins the WPR approach where the focus is on the practices and relations that *produce* "problems", "subjects", "objects", and "places" (see Part II). As mentioned in Chapter 2, in a WPR analysis the conventional view that policy *addresses* "problems that exist" is challenged. In the place of this perspective, the WPR approach describes policy as *productive*, creating or constituting "problems" as particular sorts of problems (see Chapter 4).

Policies also produce "subjects" (see Chapter 5). In so doing, policies involve relations of power. As Massumi (interview in Zournazi 2002) says: "The true power of the law [and of policy] is the power to form us. It puts the paths in us. . . . " For example, Bacchi (2016a) and Bacchi and Eveline

(2010) describe policies as gendering, meaning that they actively produce what it is possible for "women" and "men" to become as "subjects". Judith Butler (1993) uses the language of "performativity" to capture the focus on the "doing" of gender. In poststructural discourse theory, "a performative is that which enacts or brings about what it names" (de Goede 2006: 10). With this understanding, people's identities "do not precede their performances, but are constituted in and through them" (Mol 2002: 38). Identity is not something that is given; it is something that is practiced: "The pervasive and mundane acts in which this is done make people what they are" (Mol 2002: 39).

Since people's identities do not "precede their performances", something other than an actor-centered form of analysis is required. Foucault (1990a: 94) describes power relations as "both intentional and non-subjective". People, he suggests, do not operate in a dream-like state. Will and calculation are involved. "The overall effect, however, escapes the actors' intentions, as well as those of anybody else" (Dreyfus and Rabinow 1983: 187). In Foucault's words, "People know what they do; they frequently know why they do what they do; but what they don't know is what what they do does" (personal communication in Dreyfus and Rabinow 1983: 187). Instead of focusing on actors and their intentions, therefore, poststructural policy analysis inquires into the practices and knowledges that produce "subjects" as particular kinds of provisional beings (see "Subjectification, Subject Positions, and Dividing Practices").

This theoretical insight applies to "objects" as well as to "subjects" (see Chapter 6). For example, Aitken (2006) makes the point that "the financial economy" is better understood "not as an exploitative system designed by particular interests, but as a performative practice, the reiteration of which in the space of everyday life makes capital possible" (de Goede 2006: 9). Instead of some monolith—"the economy"—understood to "drive" social conditions and lives, a myriad of micropractices requires repetition on a regular basis to "enact" social relations. The need for repetition confirms the contingency of those relations, and opens up the possibility of challenge and change.

Geographical "places" are produced as specific kinds of "objects" (see Chapter 7). The "nation-state", which operates as a fixed category in mainstream political science and in almost all examples of comparative politics, is only the most obvious of these creations (Rönnblom 2012). As a poststructural challenge to this impression of inevitability and stability, Rowse (2009: 45), drawing on Law (2004: 144), suggests that "nation-states" be reconceptualized as methods for assembling power relations. Such an intervention, he contends, provides a step toward problematizing sovereignty in world politics (see de Goede 2006). Other scholars (Fraser, Moore and Keane 2014; Walters 2009) adopt the poststructural practice of "gerunding"—using verb forms instead of nouns—in order to keep attention on how "things" are continually being made with the effect of opening up space for change (e.g., see gendering, earlier; see also "addict*ing*" in Chapter 6 and "border*ing*" in Chapter 7).

The relation between power and knowledge figures centrally in Foucault-influenced poststructural policy analysis. Knowledge, for Foucault, is not "truth" but what is "in the true", what is accepted as true. "Techniques of knowledge" and "strategies of power" are "joined together" in *discourse* (see "Discourses and Discursive Practices"), forming "'local centres' of power-knowledge" (Foucault 1990a: 98). The task becomes identifying the "most immediate, the most local power relations at work": "How did they make possible these kinds of discourses, and conversely, how were these discourses used to support power relations?" (Foucault 1990a: 97).

Because power is not a "thing", resistance cannot be its opposite; rather, "points of resistance are present everywhere in the power network" (Foucault 1990a: 95). This resistance operates at the microlevel: "in the transgression and contestation of societal norms; in the disruption of metanarratives of humanism;...in the 're-appearance' of 'local popular', 'disqualified', and 'subjugated knowledges'; and in the aesthetic of self-creation" (Kulynych 1997: 328).

Moreover, because there is no outside to power, resistance is necessarily implicated in methods of governing and "networks of governmentality"—"the processes implemented for conducting others" (Foucault 2009: 268) (see "Governmentality: Rationalities and Technologies"). For example, counter-conducts, a term used to describe struggle against forms of governmentality, simultaneously challenge and reinforce dominant power relations (Death 2010: 239). The place of resistance in power relations is a central consideration in Questions 3 and 6 of the WPR approach (see Chart on p. 20 in Chapter 2).

For Foucault (1990a: 92, 94), power is "exercised from innumerable points, in the interplay of nonegalitarian and mobile relations" and involves "ceaseless struggles and confrontations". Approaching power in this way as heterogeneous strategic relations highlights both the possibility and complexity of challenge and change. It also brings attention to the place of practices in producing what it is possible for us to be and how we live.

Practices, Events, and Relations

Each of the three concepts discussed in this section of the chapter—practices, events, and relations—signals the emphasis in Foucault-influenced poststructuralism on "doing", heterogeneity, and contingency. We begin with the "turn to practice" in social theory, which can be traced back to the 1960s. Since that time there have been numerous incarnations of the concept "practice" (Postill 2010; Schatzki 2001). Gherardi (2009: 118) makes a useful distinction between conceptualizing practices "from the outside", which directs attention to how *people* (in context) "do" practices, and conceptualizing practices "from the inside", which rests on a posthumanist analytic in which *practices* "do" (constitute) "subjects". Interpretive policy analysts, who focus on training policy workers to develop skills of rhetoric and persuasion (see "Problematizing, Problematizations, Self-Problematization"), tend to follow the first path, whereas Foucault-influenced poststructuralists follow the second (Ezzamel and Willmott 2009: 100). For the latter, the goal is to "decenter" the "subject".

In this view, there is "no essential, natural or inevitable way of grouping or classifying people" (Tamboukou 1999: 208). Rather, practices constitute "subjects" as particular kinds of contingent beings. Previously, we gave the example of how policy practices actively *gender* "women" and "men". Due to the proliferation of practices, gender*ing* is an ongoing process. We are never completely "gendered". Rather, we are always "becoming" "women" and "men", which creates spaces for challenge and change (Eveline 2005). Part II of the book provides other examples of this "doing" of differentiation (see Dhamoon 2011; see discussion of dividing practices, later).

Foucault (1991b: 75) describes practices as "places" where "what is said and what is done, rules imposed and reasons given, the planned and the taken for granted meet and interconnect". There is no "prime mover" in history, such as the relations of production (Veyne 1997: 156). There are only practices, local and dispersed—a "micro-physics of power" (Foucault 1979: 26). Attention is directed precisely to "*what* is done"—"what they [men (sic)] do and the way they do it" (Foucault 1984b: 48)—rather than to the motives or intentions of people. A similar analytic strategy is applied to discourse as "*what* is said", discussed in the next section. The task becomes investigating *how* it was possible to *do* those things (or to *say* those things), "constructing their external relations of intelligibility" and the knowledges (discourses) upon which they rely (Foucault 1991b: 77).

As with "subjects", "objects" do not exist as essences; they emerge as "objects for thought" in practices. For example, to understand how "madness" was produced as an "object for thought", it is necessary to examine the following practices:

> how madmen [sic] were recognized, set aside, excluded from society, interned, and treated; what institutions were meant to take them in and keep them there, sometimes caring for them; what authorities decided on their madness, and in accordance with what criteria; what methods were set in place to constrain them, punish them, or cure them; in short, what was the network of institutions and practices in which the madman [sic] was simultaneously caught and defined. (Foucault 1969 in Eribon 1991: p. 214)

Here, Foucault is not questioning the existence of something "real" that is being regulated; however, this "thing" is not "madness" until it is produced through the practices he describes. As Veyne (1997: 160) explains: "[T]here are no natural objects.... There are only multiple objectivizations ('population', 'fauna', 'subjects under law'), correlatives of heterogeneous practices". Chapter 6 offers examples of the "making" and "unmaking" of "objects" (or "objectivizations") in policy work.

In this way of thinking, the emphasis shifts from presumed objects to the *relations* involved in their becoming. Relations, and networks of relations, *replace* objects (Veyne 1997: 181), as illustrated in the previous section of this chapter with the shift in focus from power as a *thing* to *power relations*. Hence, the analytic target becomes the "connections, encounters, supports, blockages, plays of forces, strategies and so on", in order "to show that things 'weren't as necessary as all that'" (Foucault 1991b: 76).

Importantly, this analytic strategy challenges conventional views of causality, in which one thing (or a few things) causes another. Instead, Foucault effects "a sort of multiplication or pluralization of causes" (Foucault 1991b: 76), a proliferation of "events" as the random results of "the interweaving of relations of power and domination" (Tamboukou 1999: 207). "Everything depends on everything else" (Veyne 1997: 170). Foucault focuses on "events" as a way of "making visible a *singularity* at places where there is a temptation to invoke a historical constant, an immediate anthropological trait, or an obviousness which imposes itself uniformly on all" (Foucault 1991b: 76; emphasis in original). "Events", as conceptualized here, form an important part of genealogy (see later).

To undertake this kind of analysis Foucault recommends starting from "practical texts", "the supposedly minor texts of those who actually made policy and wielded power" (Rabinow 2003: 49). These policy texts, he tells us, introduce "programmes of conduct" (Foucault 1991b: 75), "written for the purpose of offering rules, opinion, and advice on how to behave as one should". They are themselves the "objects of a 'practice'", intended to "constitute the eventual framework of everyday conduct" (Foucault 1986: 12–13). Such practices comprise "the leading edges of governmental problematization" (Osborne 1997: 176). The study of modes of problematization within these texts makes it possible to analyze "questions of general import"—our relations to things, to others and to ourselves—"in their historically unique form" (Foucault 1984b: 49).

It is precisely this mode of analysis that the WPR approach encourages and facilitates. As explained in Chapter 2 its object of analysis is "prescriptive texts". It targets the full range of governmental practices, including instruments, techniques, programs and policies. "Government" is understood in the broad sense associated with a governmentality approach (see later) to embrace the wide gamut of agencies, professionals, and experts involved in conducting conduct.

The questions the WPR approach brings to "practical texts" make it possible to identify and interrogate governmental problematizations via these understandings of practices, events, and relations (see WPR Chart on page 20). Question 2 constructs "their external relations of intelligibility" (see earlier), emphasizing the place of knowledges (discourses) in governing practices. Question 3 traces the "connections, encounters, supports, blockages, plays of forces, strategies and so on" (see quote earlier). Questions 4 and 5 consider the effects produced by specific problematizations, such as the creation of "objects" and "subjects". Question 6 attends to "ceaseless struggles and confrontations" in the "interplay of nonegalitarian and mobile relations" (Foucault 1990a: 92, 94; see "Power, Knowledge, and Resistance"). The WPR approach also recognizes research and policy analysis as political practices, requiring that policy workers/analysts apply its questions to their own proposals, in a practice of self-problematization.

Discourses and Discursive Practices

The term *discourse* proliferates in contemporary policy analysis and social theory, with diverse meanings, even *among* poststructuralists. Commonly, poststructuralism is associated with the "linguistic turn", and the proposition that "it is through language that knowledge and, indeed, reality are constituted" (Carter 2013: 583). However, Foucault explicitly distanced himself from studies that focused on linguistics and communication. In *The Archaeology of Knowledge*, he states:

> Discourse, at least as analysed by archaeology, that is, at the level of its positivity, is not a consciousness that embodies its project in the external form of language (*langage*); it is not a language (*langue*), plus a subject to speak it. It is a practice that has its own forms of sequence and succession. (Foucault 1972: 169)

Adopting this stance, this book sits at a critical distance from forms of discourse analysis that focus on patterns of speech, rhetoric, and communication, such as critical discourse analysis and interpretive approaches.

Following Foucault, discourses are understood as *socially produced forms of knowledge* that set limits upon what it is possible to think, write or speak about a "given social object or practice" (McHoul and Grace 1993: 32). "Knowledge" in this context is not truth; rather, it refers to what is "in the true"—what is accepted as truth—and is understood to be a cultural product. Indeed, there is skepticism about the whole idea of producing "knowledge" in research, signaled by the use of scare quotes around the term and by references to knowledges in the plural. The significance of this challenge to knowledge as truth is indicated by the automatic underlining in red of the term *knowledges* in most software programs, suggesting misspelling of "knowledge". Questioning "knowledge" is no easy task!

In French, Foucault's first language, there are two terms for "knowledge"—*savoir* and *connaissance*. Put simply, *savoir* refers to general background "knowledge", while *connaissance* refers to specific disciplines, primarily "scientific" knowledges, such as psychiatry or economics. Foucault (1972: 15 fn 2; emphasis in original) offers the following elaboration: "*Savoir* refers to the conditions that are necessary in a particular period for this or that type of object to be given to *connaissance* and for this or that enunciation to be formulated". "Discourse", therefore, refers to *savoir*, while specific disciplines, or knowledges, become "discourses" or "discursive formations" (Foucault 1972).

Foucault's starting point for analysis is "*what* is said", the specified "enunciation" in the above quotation. He refers to these things said as *statements*, which he describes as "monuments" (Foucault 1991a: 60) or "events" (see previous section of this chapter): "a statement is always an event that neither the language (*langue*) nor the meaning can quite exhaust" (Foucault 1972: 28). This description draws attention to statements as "things" that have a material form, rather than simply some comment made in conversation. The objective is to establish discourse in its "ponderous, awesome materiality", bridging a symbolic-material division (Foucault 1972: 216).

To avoid confusion with language studies, it is important to emphasize that Foucault's interest is not in "what *people* said" but in "*what* people said", in "*exactly* what is said" (Veyne 1997: 156; emphasis in original; Bacchi and Bonham 2014). As Veyne (1997: 157) explains, "Nor is discourse ideology; it is almost the opposite. It is what is really said, unbeknownst to the speakers". The question becomes how it is possible for "*what* is said" to be "*sayable*" (Foucault 1991a: 59; emphasis in original). Here, we are directed back to discourse (knowledge)—the background epistemological and ontological assumptions—and discourses ("scientific" knowledges) that establish a statement as "in the true" and that permit "an enunciation to be formulated" (see earlier).

Together "discourse" and "discourses" comprise the "unexamined ways of thinking" (Foucault 1994a: 456) within governmental problematizations, targeted by Question 2 in a WPR analysis (see WPR Chart on page 20). For example, the notion of "skills" in labor market and industrial relations policy relies upon a vision of human beings as skill-acquiring animals. This ontological presupposition (*savoir*) affects how work is evaluated and workers categorized (see Bacchi 1999: 85–89), producing workers as "governable subjects". As an example of *connaissance*, psychiatry, through *DSM-5* (*Diagnostic and Statistical Manual of Mental Disorders*), plays an important role in shaping the categories and thinking in policy concerned with "disorders" such as alcohol "addiction" and "problem gambling" (Bacchi 2009; 2015b; see Chapter 6). The objective in Question 2 is to critically scrutinize the "knowledge" and knowledges that together constitute the "problems", "subjects", "objects", and "places" within specific policies.

Foucault emphasizes that discourse is a practice, indicated in the (from the opening paragraph of this section: "It [discourse] is a pr... that has its own forms of sequence and succession" (Foucault 1972: 169). The analytic task becomes inquiring into the mechanisms, procedures, and processes at work in producing these "forms of sequence and succession". These mechanisms and procedures form what Foucault calls a "discursive practice" or *dispositif* (Bacchi and Bonham 2014). As with Foucault's explicit distancing from language studies, a discursive practice has nothing to do with people conversing—despite the many studies that assume this meaning (see Bacchi and Bonham 2014). Rather, discursive practices comprise the multifarious practices and relations involved in producing "knowledge" and "*what* is said". Question 3 in WPR offers a genealogical mapping of the discursive practices involved in the production of specific governmental problematizations in selected policy proposals (see "Genealogy and Subjugated Knowledges").

Importantly, as practices, discourses have effects (Questions 4 and 5 in WPR). A way into studying these effects is provided in the mapping of the discursive practices—the mechanisms, procedures, etc.—involved in making some "things said" sayable. Through this analysis it becomes possible to reflect on the limits imposed on what *can be* thought or said about the issues under consideration. Further, through exposing the discursive practices at work the prospect of articulating the "unspeakable" and thinking the "unthinkable" is opened up (WPR, Question 4).

Mapping a discursive practice also facilitates identification of the mechanisms at work in the production of "subjects" and "objects". As discussed in "Subjectification, Subject Positions, and Dividing Practices", discourses operate through "enunciative modalities" that specify the spaces—the "subject positions"—that can be taken up. Because discourses are plural, complex, and inconsistent practices, "subject positions" are neither mandatory nor determinative. The production of "subjects" is pursued in Chapter 5, and the production of "objects" in Chapters 6 and 7.

As mentioned earlier, discourses bridge a symbolic-material division. They do not merely *represent* "the real"; they are part of its *production* (McHoul and Grace 1993: 35). Foucault made this point in his insistence that he was not interested solely in the formation of discourses but in "the effects in the real to which they are linked" (Foucault 1994b, in Bernauer 1992: 144). In line with this position, the WPR approach pursues a study of the "lived effects" of problem representations (WPR, Question 5).

Specifically, it attends to the ways in which "a discursive practice is attached to bodies in space" (Clifford 2001: 56). Such a perspective provides a counter to the view that, for poststructuralism, nothing exists "outside the text" (Gulson and Metcalfe 2015).

Problematizing, Problematizations, Self-Problematization

The term "to problematize" has become part of everyday speech, usually to indicate a desire to question something or to raise doubts about a particular proposition. The term has also become popular among researchers and theorists, alongside "problematizations" (Bacchi 2015a). However, these concepts are used in a variety of ways, making it challenging to understand just what is intended.

Most commonly, academics use the term "to problematize" to mean something very like the everyday understanding mentioned earlier—to put a particular interpretation or argument into question. However, when academics say that they wish to *problematize* something, they generally mean that they wish to analyze an issue or proposition *at the level of deep-seated assumptions*. For example, Alvesson and Sandberg (2013: 71) describe their "problematization methodology" as a way to critically assess assumptions and presuppositions in political and social theories. Along related lines the WPR approach to policy analysis involves a mode of problematizing that interrogates the deep-seated assumptions and presuppositions *within policies*—the "unexamined ways of thinking" that underpin "accepted practices" (Foucault 1994a: 456).

"To problematize" has another meaning, however. It can refer to the process of putting something forward as a "problem", to give a shape to something as a "problem". So, if I say that I wish to *problematize* high rates of alcohol consumption, I could mean *either* that I wish to challenge (question) those rates of consumption (the first meaning discussed), *or* that I wish to provide a particular way of conceptualizing those rates of consumption, e.g., as a "problem" of overuse by certain types of individuals, or as a "problem" of mass advertising, or as something else. Conceptualizations of "problems" tend to be referred to as *problematizations*. Within this second usage there is an important distinction among policy theorists, between interpretivists and poststructuralists, which we elaborate in this section.

Broadly speaking, those in the interpretive tradition direct attention to how policy workers engage in problematizing, and to the form of problematizations they produce. That is, interpretivists are interested in how policy workers *shape understandings of problems*—problems that, at some level, are taken to exist as real states or conditions. By contrast, those engaged in Foucault-influenced poststructural policy analysis contest the view that problems are real in some directly observable sense. Moreover, for those who adopt this approach, the focus is not on how *people* shape problematizations, but on how issues are problematized—constituted as "problems"—*within policies*. That is, policies and policy proposals are seen to *create* or produce "problems" as problems of particular types. Chapter 2 explained how this production occurs through the ways in which policy proposals contain implicit representations of "the problem" (i.e., problem representations).

The further contention among poststructuralists is that governing takes place through the ways in which issues are problematized. Critical attention, therefore, is directed to analyzing governmental problematizations—how "problems" are represented or constituted *within policies*, and how they have come to be represented in this fashion. In other words, the task becomes analyzing how "problems" are *made*. This form of analysis puts in question the common portrayal of policy as a "problem-solving" activity and an evidence-based practice. If the very nature of a "problem" is in dispute, any suggestion that all that is required is evidence about how to solve "it" seems to be sadly inadequate.

For interpretivists (Fischer 2003; Hoppe 2011), in the main, the concern is to find ways to train policy workers to *problematize* "effectively". "Effective" problematizing is generally taken to mean an ability to produce "shared problematizations" (Colebatch et al. 2010: 236) and, in that way, to cultivate consensus (Fischer 1980). To promote this outcome, interpretivists wish to endow "forensic policy analysts" with "skills of problem reframing", such as rhetoric and persuasion, in order to assist them to "avoid controversies and break deadlocks" (Hoppe 2002: 321).

By contrast a Foucault-influenced poststructural framework, such as the one in this book, offers policy workers/analysts critical analytic strategies rather than communication skills, such as training in rhetoric. The objective in poststructural policy analysis is to encourage policy analysts to critically interrogate governmental problematizations (how "problems" are constituted in policies) rather than to assist them to develop problematizations that avoid controversies. The intent, in effect, is to *trouble*, rather than to *cultivate*, consensus.

Instead of offering skills to policy workers to help them shape a "shared problematization" (as interpretivists desire), therefore, a Foucault-influenced poststructural analysis offers ways to interrogate, compare, and rethink common forms of problematization in policies and policy proposals. Examining specific policy interventions to see how the "problem" is constituted within them opens up a critical space to reflect on how governing takes place and with what effects for those so governed. Such an intervention, it is argued, potentially provides more substantive critique of extant social arrangements than interpretive approaches, which tend to be reformist in design and inclination (Bacchi 2015a).

This contrast in approaches to problematizing and problematizations between interpretivists and poststructuralists hinges, to a considerable extent, on divergent conceptions of the political "subject" (see "Subjectification, Subject Positions, and Dividing Practices"). In brief, interpretivists are located in a hermeneutic tradition that sees people's self-interpretations as central to understanding social organization. Foucault-influenced poststructuralists, by contrast, support a posthumanist analytic that questions the existence of a sovereign subject who can access "true" meaning, "the subject regarded as the pure founding authority of rationality" (Foucault 1972: 54). In the place of the sovereign subject, poststructural analysis considers how governmental problematizations produce particular kinds of provisional "subjects" (see Chapter 5).

It follows that, whereas interpretivists tend to focus on the problematizations that *people* produce, poststructural analysis interrogates the governmental problematizations that *constitute* what "subjects" can become. However, because analysts, similar to other people, tend to be located within the "unexamined ways of thinking" that underpin policy proposals, it is difficult to "stand back" and critically scrutinize those problematizations. For this reason, the WPR approach includes an undertaking for policy workers/analysts to engage in *self*-problematization, seeking out possible forms of domination in *their own* proposals and problematizations.

Foucault-influenced poststructural policy analysis, therefore, encourages policy workers/analysts to problematize (interrogate) the problematizations (deep-seated conceptualizations of "problems") in the policies and policy proposals they develop and implement. The goal is to identify limitations within, and possible deleterious consequences of, specific governmental problematizations through a process of continuous questioning and critique. An example illustrates the usefulness of this analytic strategy.

In Australia, the Government has introduced Compulsory Income Management plans, in lieu of cash transfers, for certain groups of Indigenous people and some non-Indigenous people in receipt of welfare, ensuring that a set proportion of their social security payment is spent on "essential" items, such as food and rent. From a Foucault-influenced perspective it becomes significant to point out how a proposal such as this one targets the behaviors of specific people, in effect making them the "problem". By contrast, a decision to increase welfare payments would constitute the "problem" as inadequate welfare income.

Clearly these quite different representations of "the problem" offer competing views of social relations, with Compulsory Income Management focusing on changing the *behaviors* of individuals while raising welfare income focuses on the *needs* of people. However, the key point from a poststructural perspective is the way in which governing occurs *through forms of problematization* (Bletsas 2012: 38–40). In this case, problematizing specific individual behaviors enables the targeting of an identified minority for particular forms of treatment, while the majority is encouraged to behave "normally" (see "dividing practices" later). In effect, then, governing takes place through how the issue is problematized. When considering governmental agendas, therefore, it is considered to be inadequate to ask simply, "What is the problem?" or "What works?" in relation to an assumed "problem"; rather, there is an imperative to ask "What is the problem represented to be?". Foucauldian scholars working with these ideas have provided additional insights into how governing takes place through the study of governmentality.

Governmentality: Rationalities and Technologies

The term *governmentality*, coined by Foucault (1991c), conjoins the words "govern" and "mentality". It is used in the general sense to refer to different ways of thinking about governing (govern-*mentalities*). In a more specific usage it describes a particular form of government, with origins in sixteenth-century Western Europe and characteristic of contemporary Western democracies, in which the security, reproduction, productivity, and stability of the "population" are concerns of the state. This form of government, described as "a triangle: sovereignty, discipline, and governmental management" (Foucault 2009: 143), constitutes a "bio-politics" (Foucault 2008), with "population as its target, political economy as its major form of knowledge, and apparatuses of security as its essential technical instrument". It encompasses "rationalities" and "technologies": "the ensemble formed by institutions, procedures, analyses and reflections, calculations and tactics that allow the exercise of this very specific, albeit very complex, form of power" (Foucault 2009: 144).

Foucault's lectures on governmentality produced a field of investigation described as an "analytics of government" (Dean 1999). This poststructural mode of theorizing has had a significant impact in the following areas: studies on the government of economic life, technologies of risk, postcolonial studies, histories of sexuality, and cultural studies. It offers a rethinking of many of the assumed categories and concepts in policy studies. Specifically, it eschews grand theory based on the role of "the state" or "ideology", turning instead to the routine and mundane practices involved in the "shaping of governable domains and governable persons" (Rose et al. 2006: 101).

Some feminists with poststructural sensibilities have situated their policy analysis within a governmentality perspective (for example, Smart 1996; Carrington and Watson 1996; Goodwin 1996; Cohen 2014; Prügl 2015). The state and its agencies are no longer preeminent in these analyses, and the micropractices and microsites involved in the normalizing of populations come into view. Mechanisms and technologies that "govern" gender relations that have been interrogated include: laws; public programs; official "guidelines" such as Dietary Guidelines; planning regulations and building designs; health and welfare measurement and monitoring tools; professional discourses; contact with "experts" and allied agencies; and self-surveillance (see Bordo 2003; Sanger 2008; Ristovski-Slijepcevic et al. 2010; Fernandez 2012; du Rose 2015).

To study governmentality (as contemporary government) attention is directed to "rationalities" and "technologies" in both conventional political institutions and the multiple agencies and groups (academics, professionals, experts) which contribute to societal administration. *Governmental rationalities* are the rationales produced to justify particular modes of rule, to make "some form of that activity thinkable and practicable both to its practitioners and to those upon whom it was practiced" (Gordon 1991: 3). They constitute contingent, historically formed "modalities of power", sometimes described as "diagrams of rule", which "reside on a base of human practice and human history" (Foucault 1990b: 37), not attributable to the intentions or tactics of specific individuals.

Rationalities are named in various ways depending on the particular aspect of the rationale, or way of thinking, that is emphasized. For example, Rose et al. (2006: 98; emphasis added) draw a distinction between a "broad family" of "*social* rationalities of government" that "conceive of that which is to be governed as a society of interdependent citizens and interlinked social and economic processes that are amenable to knowledge and planning" and "*postsocial* or advanced liberal rationalities", such as neoliberalism, that reject some or all of these presuppositions. Other useful studies identify "security" (Walters 2004), "unease" (Bigo 2002), "evidence-based policy" (St. Pierre 2006), and "affectivity" (Clough 2007) as political rationalities.

Importantly, rationalities are not ideal types. Rather, an analytics of government attends to the "singularity of ways of governing and conducting ourselves" (Dean 1999: 20–21). Nor are political rationalities static. Rather, they are constantly undergoing modification, while retaining certain "styles of thought and technological preferences" (Rose et al. 2006: 98). Further, there is no assumption that the "mere existence of a diagram of government" *determines* outcomes, which would ignore "governmentality's genealogical foundations and thus its emphasis on the contingent and invented (and thus always mutable) nature of governmental thought and technique" (Rose et al. 2006: 99; see next section on genealogy). With power understood to be both productive and dispersed, resistance becomes possible (see Death 2006).

Political rationalities draw upon the theories, ideas, philosophies, and forms of knowledge that characterize our intellectual heritage. In contemporary liberal policies, for example, "these mentalities are often derived from the human sciences (such as psychology, economics and medicine)" (Dean 1999: 16). Through this lens the scope of governing is broadened beyond conventional political institutions to recognize the role of such knowledges, or discourses, as governing practices. Identifying and analyzing governmental rationalities, therefore, encourages a questioning of forms of thinking ("unexamined ways of thinking"; Foucault 1994a: 456) that guide and shape how governing takes place and what it is possible for us to become. It also allows us to see how governing may take place "at a distance" (Miller and Rose 1990: 9) through forms of discipline and regulation that establish societal norms. Such norms incite the production of "governable subjects" who engage in self-surveillance and self-regulation, a topic pursued in the section on subjectification (see later).

"Technologies" encompass the mechanisms through which governing takes place, including specific instruments such as censuses, league tables, performance data, and case management, and the vast array of programs and policies produced to shape the conduct of individuals and groups. Rowse (2009), for example, illustrates how governing takes place *through numbers* (Rose 1991; Miller 2001). He explores how the current Australian census arranges the "population" into categories (such as Indigenous and non-Indigenous) with repercussions for the sorts of political claims that can be made. Because a census rests on certain key and contestable assumptions (e.g., the "reality" of "nation-states") and has contestable political effects, it ought to be viewed, Rowse suggests, as a political technology that shapes political possibilities, rather than as a neutral, statistical register.

Technologies tend to reflect specific political rationalities. Harris (1999: 34) offers the example of social security programs as governing mechanisms, which "incorporate certain theories about the level of income needed to safeguard against unjustifiable hardship, suppositions about the relationships between equity, redistribution and competition, and notions about work incentive and benefit levels". However, technologies are not simply the "handmaidens" of rationalities. Henman (2006), for example, shows how ICTs (Information and Communications Technologies) shape what it is possible to think and hence plan or organize in the way of governing. Technologies, thus, form part of an ontological politics (Mol 1999) that enables some realities and disables others, highlighting the imperative to consider how this occurs.

Political vocabulary can be usefully viewed as a governmental technology for its role in making "politics thinkable" (Dean 1999: 44–45). Reflecting Foucault's nominalism (1990a: 93) and Tanesini's (1994) view of concepts as proposals, categories such as "labor", "capital", "productivity", "welfare dependency", and even "economy" need to be studied in relation to their emergence (see "Genealogy and Subjugated Knowledges") and in terms of their effects. This approach to vocabulary contests the tendency in realist sociology and much social policy to adopt these and similar concepts as "self-evident descriptors of the terrain being analysed" (Larner 2008: 23). By contrast, in governmentality studies, reflecting a poststructural sensibility, categories, and concepts are "denaturalised, made specific and their governmental implications revealed" (Larner 2008: 23; see discussion in Chapter 6).

Problematizations play a prominent role in the study of governmentality. As Dean (1999: 27) describes, the key starting point of an analytics of government is a "problematization", the action of calling into question some aspect of the "conduct of conduct". Of particular interest are "family resemblances" in "modes of problem formation" (Rose et al. 2006: 88), which enable the identification of specific political rationalities. For example, Dean and Hindess (1998: 9) describe a neoliberal "mentality of rule" as "a style of problematisation, a mode of reasoning that can best be identified by examining problematisations". A critical analytic task becomes discerning "which of these problematizations indicate lines of fracture and transformation and which indicate a consolidation of regimes of government" (Dean 1999: 44).

The WPR approach shares basic premises with a governmentality perspective, specifically:

- a conception of governing as including but beyond the state;
- a rejection of grand theorizing in favor of a focus on singular "events" and mundane practices;
- a conception of power as relational and productive;
- the centrality of knowledges (discourses) in governing processes;
- the usefulness of identifying "family resemblances" among problematizations to characterize political rationalities;
- the usefulness of comparisons among problematizations for making judgments about potential deleterious effects;
- a genealogical focus; and
- a view of "subjects" as constituted in practices.

It provides a "tool" to interrogate the problematizations in policies, programs, and other governmental technologies with the goal of destabilizing taken-for-granted ways of thinking about and doing politics. The next section pursues the significance of genealogy as a part of this analysis.

Genealogy and Subjugated Knowledges

Genealogy, in Foucault, brings social criticism together with a particular approach to history, described later. It is important to distinguish Foucauldian genealogy from the family history project of attempting to trace a line of descent from an ancestor. For Foucault, relying on

Nietzsche, genealogies are records of *discontinuity*, of twists and turns, of skeletons in the closet (if you will).

One goal, thus achieved, is the de-inevitabilization of the present, so that "the things which seem most evident to us" are recognized as contingent, "always formed in the confluence of encounters and chances, during the course of a precarious and fragile history" (Foucault 1990b: 37). Beyond demonstrating that present practices are contingent, the intent is to show "how these practices contingently emerged" (Koopman 2013: 141). "Emergence", for Foucault, refers not to origins or causality, but to the "moment of arising", the "entry of forces", and the "endlessly repeated play of dominations" (Foucault 1977: 148–150).

Where Foucauldian *archaeology* draws attention to the embedded knowledges ("unexamined ways of thinking"; Foucault 1994a: 456) that underpin contemporary practices, *genealogy* highlights the battles that take place over knowledge. In this view, there is no universal basis for truth. Rather, truth and knowledge are *produced* in "'local centres' of power-knowledge" (Foucault 1990a: 98). Genealogy, then, is concerned with the multitudes of practices—the "processes, procedures and apparatuses" (Tamboukou 1999: 202)—involved in the production of "truth".

To this end, Foucault (1990c: 262) endorses the need for a "history of the present", in which he "sets out" from "a problem expressed in the terms current today". This form of history does not work backwards from the perspective of current beliefs or values; rather, it rejects any presumption that the present is "a necessary endpoint or outcome of the trajectories it seeks to chart" (Dean 2002: 217). These trajectories are intelligible expositions of events, discourses, and practices, "the articulation of the series of practices . . . that accounts for our current practices" (Flynn 2006: 40). For example, one could examine abortion practices in a specific site today and look to the past to identify practices (e.g., the status and role of the medical profession) that contribute to an account of the current situation (see Bacchi 1999).

Again, there is no intention here of tracing a direct path of "influence". Rather, the emphasis is on the heterogeneity of practices, which means that another path *could have* been followed. This heterogeneity is captured in the *event*, a term Foucault borrowed from conventional history and reworked. Events are not simply bits of data; they need to be analyzed in terms of the practices that give rise to them (see "Practices, Events, and Relations"). Events are pluralized—practices are events, statements are events—to further disrupt a linear historical account; however, only those events relevant to the issue under scrutiny need to be investigated (Tamboukou 1999: 207). The goal of this form of analysis, mentioned earlier, is to de-inevitabilize the present or, in Dean's (1999: 44) words, to render the "past as a strange land". As Dean explains, such a history sharpens the "contingency and singularity of the present" and removes our self-assurance that lives have always been lived in pretty much the same way.

At the same time, genealogies can make the unfamiliar familiar. They can indicate that the past is not so different from today in certain respects, that there are "awkward continuities" (Dean 1999: 45) and "improbable continuums" (Deleuze 1992: 35). For example, Walters (2006) shows how developments such as ID cards buy into some long-standing historical logics, including a "securitization" of national borders. The objective here is to avoid overstating the novelty of the present and so to "lessen the hold which apparently inexorable processes and master narratives like 'globalization' and 'neoliberalism' still exercise upon our political imagination" (Walters 2006: 182).

Genealogy insists that *everything* has a history, providing support for the poststructural challenge to essentialist (possessing an essence) things and forms of "being" (see Chapter 2). Foucault (1991b: 86) describes how genealogy writes the history "of the 'objectification' of those elements which historians consider as objectively given". If such elements *are made* as "objects", they can be *unmade* (see Chapter 6). Genealogy also destabilizes essentialist conceptions of "subjects". In Foucault's (1977: 153) words, "it places within a process of development everything considered immortal in man". Both the body and the "self" are rendered historical and thus mutable. As a consequence, coherent identities, both individual and collective, are disrupted (Brown 1998: 36).

Concepts are likewise historicized, reminding us to reflect on whether the concepts we deploy are "located in another knowledge and time" (Dean 1999: 45). For Foucault (1977: 152), the role of genealogy is to record "the history of morals, ideals, and metaphysical concepts, the history of the concept of liberty or of the ascetic life", making them appear as no more (and no less) than "events on the stage of historical process".

Foucault (1977: 153) describes genealogy as "effective history" because it lacks "constants" and "introduces discontinuity into our very being". It achieves this effect through allowing "an insurrection of subjugated knowledges" against established scientific discourse (Foucault 2003: 7, 9). Subjugated knowledges consist of "historical knowledges" that "have been buried or masked" by "functional arrangements or systematic organizations", and

> a whole series of knowledges that have been disqualified as nonconceptual knowledges, as insufficiently elaborated knowledges: naïve knowledges, hierarchically inferior knowledges, knowledges that are below the required level of erudition or scientificity. (Foucault 2003: 7)

In the latter category, Foucault (1980: 82) includes the knowledges of the psychiatric patient, the ill person, the nurse, and the delinquent. This stance indicates Foucault's alignment with "outsiders"—"the prisoner, the exile, the 'abnormal'" (Flynn 1989: 196).

Foucault's (1980: 83) concern is the *tactical usefulness* rather than the *content* of subjugated knowledges. The aim, through genealogies, is to *play off* subjugated knowledges against "the rights of a science that is in the hands of the few" (Foucault 2003: 7). A contemporary example is Death's (2006: 416) challenge to the rejection of subaltern Indigenous knowledges in Environmental Impact Assessments in South Africa. The "re-appearance" of subjugated knowledges enables resistance at the "micro-level" (Death 2010: 28) and construction of a "counter-memory" (Foucault 1977: 160).

Foucault (1986: 11–12) clearly explains the place of genealogy in the study of problematizations: "The archaeological dimension of the analysis made it possible to examine the forms [of problematization] themselves; its genealogical dimension enabled me to analyze their formation out of the practices and the modifications undergone by the latter". Question 3 in a WPR approach creates the space to perform genealogical analyses of identified problem representations, "mapping" the heterogeneous practices from which they emerge. It also encourages the comparison of problematizations and their genealogies across space and time to further destabilize what appears to be self-evident (Bacchi 2012). Question 6 ensures attention is paid to the battles that take place *over* knowledge.

There are, however, challenges involved in adopting genealogy as an analytic intervention. Foucault (1977: 139) describes genealogy as "gray, meticulous and patiently documentary": "it must record the singularity of events outside any monotonous finality". Walters (2006: 174) suggests that policy analysts who wish to engage in genealogy as a form of critique use "diagrams" (e.g., Ewald 1991, on insurance), to grasp "provisional coherence" in a "polytemporal and non-linear form of policy studies".

Genealogically inspired questions, such as the following, could also accompany one's analysis:

- What types of knowledge are disqualified in the problem representation under study?
- Which "objects" have been produced ("objectified")?
- Which culture-bound concepts require a history?
- What kinds of political "subjects" are elicited? Which are diminished?

Subjectification, Subject Positions, and Dividing Practices

Subjectification refers to the production, or *making*, of provisional "subjects" of particular kinds through policy practices (see Chapter 5). It includes the characteristics, behaviors and dispositions that political "subjects" are encouraged to adopt and how they may develop in relation to those "repertoires of conduct" (Rose 2000: 43). The "subject" in this view is an effect of politics, always in process, and a product of power-knowledge relations (Golder 2010). This way of thinking about political "subjects"—as *made* and *becoming*—puts in question conventional notions of an unchanging human essence, commonly associated with the rational, autonomous individual of Enlightenment humanism. Foucault (1972: 227) discredits the notion of a "founding subject" who is "beyond time". In its place are "subjects" who are thoroughly contingent—emergent, constituted or produced, "in formation" (Bonham et al. 2015).

Conceptions of political subjectivity are highly relevant to policy analysis, primarily because assumptions about human nature commonly underpin policy proposals. For example, in the Australian government plan to "change" citizen behaviors, a universal, rational, autonomous and self-interested subject is readily identifiable: "People assess the choice before them in terms of costs and benefits and then select the choice that maximizes their net benefits" (Australian Government 2007: 7). Similarly, situational crime prevention proposals to enhance street lighting rest on premises about how "rational actors" will behave in certain circumstances (Tilley 2010).

Poststructural policy analysis highlights the importance of identifying contingent ontological presuppositions, such as those just cited, in governmental problematizations as a way of encouraging a rethinking of specific policies and programs that rest on such unquestioned premises

(Question 2, WPR approach). Further, it emphasizes how policies (broadly understood) play significant roles in *subjectification* processes, shaping ways for people to be that can be harmful and limiting (Question 5, WPR approach). Policies, it is claimed, are not simply reactions to "people who exist", conceptualized as unchanging and essential. Rather, policies are involved in shaping what it is possible for people to become, illustrating how power is a productive force (see "Power, Knowledge, and Resistance").

Governmentality studies (see earlier) are particularly concerned with governmental practices that constitute political "subjects" as "governable" through promoting identities that "perform" behaviors deemed to be desirable. Thinking about such normalizing practices as constitutive of "subjects" offers valuable insights into contemporary politics. Larner (2000: 19), for example, suggests that such an analytic approach would help explain how "economic identities have come to be posited as a new basis for political life, usurping those associated with social citizenship".

There is no implied conspiracy in this form of analysis. Nor do regimes of government *determine* the kinds of "subjects" we become. Rather, they "elicit, promote, facilitate, foster and attribute various capacities, qualities and statuses to particular agents" (Dean 1999: 32). Refusal is commonplace. As Inda (2005: 10–11) describes, "while governmental practices might seek to create specific types of subjects, it does not mean that they necessarily or completely succeed in doing so. Individuals can and do negotiate the processes to which they are subjected". For example, Mitchell's (2006) research on attempts to use education to produce a disciplined, entrepreneurial European citizen found that the students she interviewed were (simply) uninterested. They preferred to describe themselves as "Marseillais".[1] On this basis, Mitchell concludes that neoliberal governmentality, as a project of "government at a distance", remains "partial and fragmentary". The reluctance of people using public services in England to identify themselves as consumers or customers of public services supports this view (Clarke and Newman 2009).

The constitutive effects of protest and resistance practices, and the place of bodies in those practices (Foucault 1977: 153), also need to be recognized. For example, Death (2010: 245) emphasizes how, through the embodied practices of protest, such as hunger strikes, sit-ins, and civil disobedience, "new identities and subjectivities are performatively constituted". At the same time, it is important to be wary of attributing "agency", in the sense of independent moral capacity, to "subjects". Rather, "subjects" need to be thought about in terms of their location within plural and contradictory discourses, which opens up spaces for challenge.

History, or more specifically genealogy (Question 3, WPR approach; see preceding section), provides a useful device for dispelling the view that "there are universals which animate the conduct and experience of human beings in every age" (Dean 1999: 45). As Foucault (1990b: 23) tells us, "There is a history of the subject just as there is a history of reason". Genealogy "maps" the heterogeneous procedures and practices at work in the production of always-provisional "subjects".

In 1982 Foucault (2000: 326) declared that the goal of his work over the previous 20 years had been to "create a history of the different modes by which, in our culture, human beings are made subjects". He describes three interacting "modes of objectification that transform human beings into subjects". Each offers a fertile field for genealogical research:

1. *The role of authoritative knowledges in delineating how "subjects" ought to be, through the production of norms.* Foucault emphasizes the diverse and at times contradictory subject statuses endorsed and promoted in various discourses (knowledges): for example, the sexual subject (psychology, psychiatry, etc.); the productive subject (economics, accounting, etc.); and the healthy subject (medicine, physiology, etc.). Tensions among these statuses create room for contestation.
2. *The place of dividing practices in producing "subjects".* Dividing practices are dynamic practices of differentiation and subordination, which prove to be vital governing mechanisms. They often target minorities or groups identifiable in terms of "race"/ethnicity, class, gender, and sexuality. Examples include citizen/migrant, youth/adult, responsible/irresponsible, man/woman, disabled/fit, welfare recipient/tax payer, etc.

   The construction of opposition between groups (e.g., between the "responsible gambler" and the "problem gambler") works to promote desired behaviors among the general population, making them "governable" (Race 2005). As Valverde (1998) explains, we are governed through a belief that self-control is freedom and that those who "fail" to display this characteristic, e.g., gambling "addicts", "the obese", need to be monitored and at times punished. This form of governing provides a *dramatized version* of failure that leaves us convinced that we are free while our behaviors are regulated/defined in part by this marking of "others" as deficient in some way and through other sets of relations, especially through the culture of consumption.

3. *The ways "a human being turns him- or herself into a subject"* (Foucault 2000: 327). The target of analysis here becomes the "enunciative modalities", i.e., statuses, sites, and positions, in a discursive practice that makes "being" a "subject" possible (Clifford 2001: 54–58; see "Discourses and Discursive Practices"). For example, to become a legitimate "subject" in a specific policy field, one must take up the appropriate subject position in a discourse, e.g., "welfare recipient", "problem gambler", "asylum seeker", with its accompanying associations and implications. Subject positions are not fixed, however; they are precarious, contradictory and always in process (Weedon 1987: 33).

Late in his life Foucault (1986: 10) came to highlight the usefulness of analyzing problematizations to explore how people become "subjects"—studying "the conditions in which human beings 'problematize' what they are, what they do, and the world in which they live". Through Question 5 the WPR approach prompts exactly this form of interrogation. It asks how "subjects" are produced as particular kinds of subjects within identified governmental problematizations, and considers the possible impacts on perceptions of self and others.

As discussed in Chapter 2, the task of identifying governmental problematizations is particularly challenging given the immersion of analysts in the governing logics and knowledges of the time. However, as seen earlier, subjectification effects are not determined. Moreover, subject positions are plural and contradictory, creating space for challenge. The WPR approach serves to expand that space through the undertaking to apply its questions to one's own proposals for change (see WPR Chart on page 20). This analytic commitment to self-problematization creates an opportunity to "recognize the optionality and nonessentiality of a particular way of being" (Clifford 2001: 133), allowing one to think differently (Foucault 1986: 8).

A Foucault-influenced poststructural approach to policy analysis involves modes of inquiry that proceed from specific conceptions of power, knowledge, resistance, and discourse. Poststructural policy analysis requires analytic attention to productive activities: practices, events and relations, subjectification and dividing practices, and problematization, including self-problematization. The WPR approach provides a strategy that enables policy analysts to interrogate *policies as productive (or constitutive)—making "things" come to be.* The distinct intellectual stance outlined in this chapter is drawn into a set of user-friendly questions that can be applied in regular policy analysis practices. In Part II of the book we contextualize and describe the outcomes of various WPR projects (in a range of countries, in a range of fields) under key themes: making and unmaking "problems"; making and unmaking "subjects"; making and unmaking "objects"; and making and unmaking "places". The examples of WPR applications provided in Part II demonstrate the utility of this analytic strategy as a tool for critique.

Note

1. For a poststructuralist it is important to note that the interviewed students remain within discourse, here adopting the subject position of "Marseillais" or from Marseilles, France. See Appendix.

PART II

Interrogating Policies as Constitutive: WPR Applications

CHAPTER 4

Making and Unmaking "problems"

Abstract This chapter pursues a central task in the book, explaining what is accomplished by focusing on how policies produce or constitute "problems". To begin, it canvasses how "problems" are conceptualized in classic rationalist, and in more recent interpretive and critical realist approaches to policy analysis, and indicates the possible deleterious implications of assuming the existence of problems as objective and uncontroversial states. Second, the chapter draws on WPR applications in two policy areas—alcohol and drugs policy and gender equality policy—to show how the interrogation of problematizations provides important insights into how governing takes place. In this way it illustrates the distinctive contribution of a poststructural questioning of "problems".

Keywords "social problems" · "wicked problems" · rationalism · framing · "gender equality" · "alcohol problems"

This chapter and the other chapters in this part of the book introduce selected applications of the WPR approach to indicate how policy workers/analysts in many countries have used it to query conventional ways of thinking about policy development, and to draw attention to the constitutive, or productive, character of policy. It draws on articles, books, and theses that focus on the question: "What's the Problem Represented to be?" The goal is to illustrate just what this question accomplishes in terms

C. Bacchi, S. Goodwin, *Poststructural Policy Analysis*,
DOI 10.1057/978-1-137-52546-8_4

of political analysis and how it can be useful to those who develop, implement, and evaluate policy. The chapter covers two topic areas: alcohol and other drug use, and "gender equality", including gender mainstreaming, parental leave, and violence against women.

Prior to introducing these topics and the related applications it is important to establish the basis of the premise in WPR that the concept "problem" needs to be problematized. The term is ubiquitous in discussions of policy and elsewhere: in public debate, political commentary, and in the media. One needs only to listen to any public affairs program or indeed to almost any speech by a parliamentarian to hear the term being used as if its meaning is clear and uncontentious. In this view, there are (simply) *problems that exist*, which must be dealt with!

Moreover, the concept "problem" holds a privileged place both in political theory (Shapiro 2002; Glynos and Howarth 2007) and in the field of policy analysis itself, with contrasting positions reflecting specific historical contexts. As we shall see below, the term "problem" is also deployed unproblematically in specific policy areas, for example, in reference to "alcohol problems" and the "drugs problem". And yet, wide-ranging meanings, which usually carry a negative valence, are ascribed to the term. For example, it can signal a worry or concern (Turnbull 2005: 238), a puzzle, or "a gap between a current situation and a more desirable one" (Hoppe 2011: 23). In this situation, it becomes critically important to consider how the concept "problem" operates in various policy approaches and the implications of different meanings for policy workers *cum* analysts.

Understandings of "problems" in Policy Analysis

For simplicity's sake, it is possible to identify two broad traditions in the literature on policy development—comprehensive rationalism and political rationalism—with links to current perspectives. As described below, we see echoes of the former in policy cycle models and evidence-based policy, and of the latter in interpretivism.

Classic rationalist approaches to policy studies, such as Herbert Simon's (1961: 23) comprehensive or technical rationalism, developed in the 1940s, assume "a given set of problems". The job of analysts in these models is (simply) to find the appropriate means to achieve objectives set by legislatures in their response to those *given* problems. This formalistic approach to policy-making is reflected in the classic heuristic for understanding the policy process as four (or sometimes more) "stages" in a "policy cycle": agenda-setting, policy formulation, policy implementation, and evaluation. Developed initially by Lasswell (1956), this template has attracted a good deal of criticism (Jann and Wegrich 2007). However, it is still readily adopted as a way to conceive the broad parameters of policy development (WHO 2015: 49–50). The first stage in the cycle, agenda setting, presumes a preliminary step of "problem identification" or "problem recognition". The clear presumption is that problems exist as independent entities that need only to be identified or recognized. Reflecting this view Jann and Wegrich (2007: 45) state: "Policy-making presupposes the recognition of a policy problem. Problem recognition itself requires that a social problem has been defined as such and that the necessity of state intervention has been expressed".

In the "stages" heuristic, therefore, the purpose of policy interventions is to *solve* "problems that exist". This thinking is closely associated with evidence-based policy models, which currently hold near-hegemonic status across a wide spectrum of countries and international organizations. In evidence-based policy, governing officials ("the government") *name* the problems upon which analysts deliver "evidence" about "what works". In this process the necessarily political contestation around how "problems" are constituted within policies is displaced, as is the meaning and interpretation of "evidence" (Bacchi 2009: 252–255). While critical realists claim to broaden the focus of analysis by asking "what works for whom in what circumstances and in what respects, and how?" (Pawson and Tilley 2004: 2), the continuing emphasis on "what works" assumes the independent existence of a problem that needs fixing (see Bacchi, 2016b).

A challenge to the proposition in comprehensive rationalism that government decision-making is simply a matter of technical expertise came from the so-called "political rationalists" of the 1970s and 1980s (see Bacchi 1999: 24–31), headed by scholars such as Lindblom (1980), Wildavsky (1979), Dery (1984), and Rein and Schön (1977). In their judgment, the plurality of expressed views on an issue means that "the *nature of the problem* is itself in doubt", making urgent "the exploration of problem setting" (Rein and Schön 1977: 237; emphasis added), "problem definition" (Dery 1984) and "problem framing" (Schön 1979). For political rationalists the interest, however, is in how to *manage* competing perspectives rather than in *interrogating* problematizations, as is pursued in a WPR analysis. The primary focus is on process. Policy analysts are assigned the role of conflict managers: "policy development is about problem setting, dilemma and tradeoff management, and consensus building via coalition formation" (Rein and Schön 1977: 237). Indeed, analysts are encouraged to match problems pragmatically to what is feasible: "in public policy...creativity consists of finding a problem about which something can and ought to be done" (Wildavsky 1979: 3).

This same focus is apparent among contemporary interpretivists, introduced in Chapter 3 (see "Problematizing, Problematizations, Self-Problematization"). This broad tradition within policy studies usefully decenters the idea of "an authoritative 'problem-solving' power-figure (that of the 'state' or 'government')" and conceptualizes a process "characterized by multiple (but connected) participants and competing perspectives" (Lancaster et al. 2014: 148). In the place of problem-solving, drawing on the work of Kingdon (2003), they describe policy-making as an "ongoing process of managing the problematic" or the "governance of problems" (Lancaster et al. 2014: 148).

However, as with the political rationalists, the emphasis remains on the process of *managing* problems rather than *interrogating* how they are conceptualized. A primary concern, for example, is training policy analysts in communication "skills" (e.g., rhetoric, persuasion) to help them *frame* problems "effectively" in order to "avoid controversies and break deadlocks" (Hoppe 2002: 321). The objective for interpretivists, as explained in Chapter 3, is to produce "forensic policy analysts" and "shared problematizations", rather than to query how "problems" are constituted (or made to be) within specific policies, which is the task undertaken in this book. A key distinction of poststructural policy analysis is the focus on critically interrogating the problematizations through which governing occurs rather than on producing "shared problematizations".

Notably, a few researchers use the language of framing to draw attention to how certain issues, such as equality and equity, are assigned different meanings in specific policy texts (Freeman 2006; Smith et al. 2009; Bambra et al. 2011). This form of analysis shares some common ground with a WPR approach due to the interest in how issues are conceptualized. However, the emphasis in these studies tends to be on the lack of fit between what governments *promise* and what they *deliver*, portraying policy as an exercise in rhetoric. By contrast, WPR does not work at the level of language or political manipulation. Rather, it creates the space to interrogate deep-seated presuppositions and assumptions—the "unexamined ways of thinking" (Foucault 1994a: 456)—that underpin policies and that can be identified through analyzing policy proposals.

Despite the clear distance between interpretivists and those who adopt more rationalist approaches (see above), for many interpretivists, a primary concern is agenda-setting. Illustrative of this emphasis on process, Kingdon (2003) highlights the central role of "policy entrepreneurs", those who take the lead in promoting a policy, and the "windows of opportunity" for advancing an agenda. Indeed, for Kingdon (2003: 109–11), a "condition" becomes a "problem" once it achieves agenda status. The primary political exercise in this case is having an issue placed on a policy agenda, downplaying consideration of how "problems" are constituted.

The prevalence of this perspective is reflected in the term "wicked problems", which has become increasingly popular among policy analysts in national and international contexts (WHO 2015; Australian Public Service Commission 2007). "Wicked problems" serves as conceptual shorthand for problems described as "messy", "fuzzy", and "complex", multicausal problems that require intersectoral interventions. At times, the language of mainstreaming is used in reference to "wicked problems", justifying the attention of several government agencies. Examples include: HiAP (Health in All Policies), environmental mainstreaming, gender mainstreaming, disability mainstreaming, HIV/AIDS mainstreaming, and Indigenous mainstreaming (Elsey et al. 2005; Kok and de Coninck 2007).

While these conceptual innovations—e.g., "wicked problems", "mainstreaming"—appear designed to increase awareness of an issue deemed worthy of widespread recognition, the language of "problem" undermines any such possible intent. As with the classic rationalists, the underlying assumption remains that it is possible and politically useful to speak of a "problem" or "problems" separate from the ways in which they are conceptualized. By contrast, in a WPR analytic strategy, policies, by their nature, consist of proposals that *constitute "problems" as problems of particular kinds*. This challenge to conventional thinking about the assumed nature of problems as clear and obvious *starting points* for policy deliberation opens up debates about what is amiss and what should be done in specific contexts in novel and wide-ranging ways. It also opens up a new space for the active involvement of policy workers/analysts in contestation over the substantive content of policies, as illustrated in the applications of WPR that follow.

Alcohol and Other Drug "problems"

As mentioned above, there are specific policy areas, where the term "problems" is used *within* policies as if its meaning is clear and transparent. Such explicit references to problems commonly appear in relation to alcohol and drug use. In 1980, the World Health Organization (WHO 1980; emphasis added) produced an expert committee report on "*problems* related to alcohol consumption". The more recent *Global Strategy on the Harmful Use of Alcohol* (WHO 2010: 8; emphasis added) calls for "raised global awareness of the magnitude and nature of the health, social and economic *problems* caused by harmful use of alcohol". As another example, the General Secretariat of the Council of the European Union describes a new Drugs Strategy as "a balanced, integrated approach to the *drugs problem*" (Council of the European Union 2004: 2; emphasis added).

Characterizing alcohol consumption and drug use as problems in this way is indicative of the long tradition within Western democracies of designating and labeling certain activities "social problems" (Bacchi 1999: 51–53). Other commonly named "social problems" include "problem gambling", teen pregnancy, and more recently obesity (Alexander and Coveney 2013). In the very labeling as "social *problems*", a kind of normative judgment is cast on these issues. Here, we have *Problems* with a capital "P", making it much more difficult to suggest (as per a WPR analysis) that the whole area needs to be rethought. As Fraser and Moore (2011: 498) note, these policies, "destined to receive close scrutiny from all sides", "are obliged to negotiate a complex political domain".

Critical analysis of the positioning of alcohol and drug use as social problems tends to draw attention to the social, structural factors that cause people to drink excessively or to take illicit drugs, as a way of reducing the stigma attached to drug "users" and "alcoholics" (Levine 1984; Sutton 1998). "Moral panic" theory (see Cohen 2002) offers a version of this argument, claiming that "the official reaction to the social condition is out of all proportion to the alleged threat" (Armstrong 2007: 427), and criticizing the tendency to target specific underprivileged groups as responsible for the problem. While these critiques usefully highlight worrisome aspects of common views on "alcohol problems", they continue to accept that such problems exist and require explanation. A WPR analytic strategy offers a different form of critique. It asks what meanings (presuppositions, assumptions, "unexamined ways of thinking", knowledges/discourses; see Chapter 2) need to be in place in order for the categories "drug problems", "alcohol problems", "gambling", or "obesity" to be intelligible, and directs attention to the practices that install those meanings (Bacchi and Bonham 2014). For example, Bacchi (2015b: 9) describes how the commonly identified "alcohol problem" of "absenteeism" relies for "problem" status on the meanings ascribed to the concepts of productivity and human capital. In this way, rather than looking for explanations (or rationalizations) for problems that are presumed to exist, genealogies of practices demonstrate how the categories of analysis (e.g., "alcohol problems", "drug problems") were *made* under specific circumstances (Bacchi 2015b), and hence, can be *unmade*.

This perspective has been taken up by analysts associated with several research institutes in Australia (e.g., National Drug Research Institute, Curtin University; The National Drug and Alcohol Research Centre, University of New South Wales), producing a "new subfield of drug policy research" (Seear and Fraser 2014: 828). Offering substantive critiques of problem-solving (Lancaster et al. 2012) and evidence-based paradigms (Lancaster 2014) that dominate the field, these analysts draw on post-structural methods of policy analysis to "acknowledge the complexities of policy and of the forces that shape its processes and outputs" (Fraser and Moore 2011: 499). They have found the WPR approach particularly helpful in this regard and have expanded its application beyond policy analysis to include case law and precedent (Seear and Fraser 2014) and content analysis of high impact law journals (Fraser and Moore 2011: 499).

In their analysis of the 1985 *Drug Misuse and Trafficking Bill* (New South Wales) Lancaster, Seear, and Treloar (2015: 1201; emphasis in original) use WPR to reflect on how constituting "illicit drug use" as an "inherently criminal activity" limits access to injecting equipment to "authorized persons", with concerning effects for population health. In this problematization, injecting equipment is produced as "both *facilitator* and *signifier* of criminality", with the effect that restrictions are placed on peer distribution of needles and syringes, and those in possession of this equipment and/or those who choose to distribute it are criminalized. As a result, the public health benefits of easier access to clean injecting equipment are undermined.

In another application of WPR, Lancaster, Duke, and Ritter (2015) produce a comparative analysis of how the "problem of drugs" is represented in "recovery" discourse in an Australian (ANCD 2012) and a

British (UKDPC 2008) report. This study highlights the importance of context to problematization. It shows how, in the UK, the notion of "recovery" is taken up and endorsed through an emphasis on individual responsibility to "recover", while the concept remains contested in Australia where drug users tend to be constituted as patients within a medical discourse. In tune with WPR, the comparison focuses on deep-seated conceptual logics rather than on the intentions of policy actors, and examines a range of possible repercussions. For example, according to the authors, despite clear differences, both problematizations have "stigmatizing and marginalizing effects" that need to be countered.

Martin and Aston's (2014) WPR analysis of how the "problem" of women's drug use is represented in high-impact law journals indicates the complexity around the matter of stigma (see du Rose 2015). They show that targeting women who use drugs as a particularly vulnerable group (given their role in reproduction, and their experience of violence) functions to "other" women in ways that can have deleterious effects. For example, access to treatment for those not so marked may be limited. At issue here are contested meanings of "gender". Although the articles that formed the basis of this study used the term "gender" (rather than "sex") "very few explored or acknowledged gender and gender differences as sociocultural constructs" (Martin and Aston 2014: 342), an issue pursued in the next section.

"Gender equality"

In most policy areas, in contrast to the drug and alcohol field, the word "problem" is not explicitly stated; rather, it is assumed. That is, recalling Osborne's (1997: 174) comment that "policy cannot get to work without first problematising its territory", all policies problematize the issues they purport to address. However, the problematizations are *implicit* within the proposals. Hence, it is necessary to start with proposals and "work backwards", as in a WPR mode of analysis, in order to "read off" how the "problem" is represented.

An apt example is "gender equality". It is uncommon to hear people talk about the "problem of gender inequality" in the same way they lament "alcohol problems". With "alcohol problems" there is an assumed non-normative behavior undermining "accepted" standards of alcohol consumption. By contrast "gender inequality" is an abstract category meant to capture wide-ranging historical and institutional processes. As a result, the meaning of the category "gender equality" is more amorphous and difficult to delineate. By examining proposals that take as their goal "gender equality", WPR provides a way to identify how the "problem" is produced or constituted as a specific sort of problem in particular contexts. Many analysts have taken up the WPR approach specifically for this purpose. Their investigations (at the time of writing) cluster around three topic areas: "gender equality" (including mainstreaming), parental leave and "work/life balance", and violence against women (domestic violence, prostitution policy). Applications relating to each topic are introduced below.

Several authors use the WPR approach to interrogate the whole notion of "gender equality". For example, Poulson's (2006: 85) project is to tease out the discourses on gender and gender equality that are in play in the International Labour Organization's (ILO) work on social dialogue. To this end, Poulson (2006: 76) raises the following questions: Which topics, issues, and problems are regarded as meaningful in the context of gender equality? "What can legitimately be thought, said, and done?" And what subject positions are available in these representations?

Poulson finds that the main "subject category" in the ILO documents she examines (1994–2003) is "The Worker". "Gender equality" is to be achieved by producing "The Woman Worker" as analogous to this category. Hence, the "problem" is represented to be women's underrepresentation in the workforce. Silences include power relations between women and men, and the "heterosexual matrix". Drawing on a postcolonial feminist perspective (see Mohanty 1991), Poulson also deploys the WPR analytic strategy to challenge the tendency in selected ILO documents to produce "Third World Women" as a static and universalized problem group set in contrast to educated, modern Western women (Poulson 2006: 154–161). Through analyzing how the "problem" of "gender equality" is represented in ILO policy, Poulson challenges the tendency to privilege paid labor and workforce status and the effects of such privileging for specific groups of women.

Calvo (2013) critically examines the European Union's (EU) gender mainstreaming strategy, with a particular focus on development cooperation and migration. She (2013: 263) emphasizes that, in the documents she studies, "gender is defined and understood as a fixed category, as a category to which a value can be assigned: either male or female". This understanding, she argues, contributes to "undermining the conceptualization and practice of gender mainstreaming" since it downplays how gender is a process entailing "relations of power and conflict". The main proposals to advance gender equality, which include employment, education, and training programs, rely on the key discourses of efficiency, independence, and labor market participation, mirroring Poulson's "Woman Worker". These individualistic problem representations are repeated in the utilitarian discourse of migration and development, where labor market "skills" are valorized over "care work" (Calvo 2013: 250).

Payne (2014) explores how the "problem" of "gender inequality" is represented in the responses of British primary care organizations (Primary Care Trusts) to mainstreaming initiatives. Deploying a WPR analytic strategy, she emphasizes how a focus on problem representations opens up spaces for policy makers to "engage with the production of 'knowledge' and the silences embedded in policy texts" (Payne 2014: 971). For example, she notes that "men's" poor health behaviors—as "more likely to smoke, use alcohol and illicit drugs, and have a poor diet" (Payne 2014: 965)—get produced as "normal masculinity", reinforcing a discourse of gender difference and constituting "men" as disadvantaged. At the same time there is "virtual silence" on the part played by external factors such as "paid and unpaid work, poverty, exclusion or the environment" on health differences (Payne 2014: 966).

Grebe (2009) examines what is referred to in Germany and other parts of Europe as "reconciliation policy", which looks to "reconcile" the assumed incompatibility between paid employment and "care work". Using WPR, Grebe (2009: 16) asks: "What is the 'incompatibility' problem represented to be?" He describes the "problem" as "socially construed in and through" four policy areas: anti-discrimination policy, childcare policy, parental leave policy and working time policy. In his view, the same "male worker model" identified by Poulson and Calvo underlies all of these areas, neglecting "the 'private' sphere and 'care work,'" and undercutting the possibility of substantive change (Grebe 2009: 121, 214).

Bjørnholt (2012) pursues the topic of work/life balance by comparing two approaches to gender equality in Norway: an experimental research project from the 1970s—the Work-Sharing Couples Project—and the current gender equality model. The former, as she describes, promoted a dual earner/dual carer model based on *part-time* paid labor and shared domestic responsibilities for both parents (assumed to be "male" and "female"). The current policy, by contrast, encourages a dual breadwinner model based on *full-time* work for both parents, supported by a "gender quota" of parental leave for men. The "problem", according to Bjørnholt (2012: 64), which was conceptualized in the 1970s to be "unequal couple relationships and the detrimental effect of patriarchal power in the family on the heterosexual love relation", has become a "problem" of "unequal parenthood" where fathers lack "rights". Comparing these problematizations allows Bjørnholt to raise for consideration the importance of reflecting on the place of domestic "care work" in conceptions of gender equality.

In relation to domestic violence, policy analysts have found the WPR questions (see WPR Chart on page 20) useful in highlighting silences in current legislative approaches. For example, Hearn and McKie (2010: 151) show that, in Finland and Scotland, the policy emphasis on securing the safety of women and their dependents, while necessary, fails to problematize the gendered nature of violence (see also Pease 2011). Individualized service provision, in their view, renders silent men's predominant role as perpetrators of violence. Along related lines Powell and Murray (2008: 465) make the case that, in Australia and New Zealand, tensions exist in how domestic violence legislation, child protection legislation, and family law construct the "problem" of domestic violence, with serious implications for child welfare. For example, the "right to contact ethos" in the Australian *Family Law Act 1975* produces domestic violence as the "exception to the norm", possibly putting some children at risk.

Carson and Edwards (2011) use a WPR analytic strategy to compare and contrast the policy and legislative approaches to prostitution and sex trafficking in Sweden and in Victoria, Australia. They note that, in Sweden, the client of prostitution is criminalized and sex trafficking is condemned. The "problem" is represented to be men's sexual desires and their "economic capacities to purchase sex and exploit women" (Carson and Edwards 2011: 77). By contrast, the Victorian harm minimization approach constitutes prostitution as tacitly acceptable "sex work" to allow for men's desires, which are perceived to be inevitable. Stressing the importance of context, the authors link these contrasting logics to different governing rationalities—in Sweden, the welfare state as protector, in Victoria, a neoliberal state committed to market relations. The point of the exercise, they propose, is not to defend one approach over the other but to tease out the complex assumptions and repercussions of the different models, providing the "potential to move beyond entrenched positions and polarised debate" (Carson and Edwards 2011: 84).

The applications of WPR in this chapter illustrate how policy workers *cum* analysts have found it a useful way to engage in critique. Their studies highlight the importance of interrogating problematizations within policies at the level of deep-seated presuppositions and assumptions, e.g., about the nature of drug use and the character of drug "users", about the meaning of "work", about sexuality and gender relations. They also emphasize the need to be attentive to the background and normative assumptions of the categories of analysis which they employ on a day-to-day basis, e.g., "drug problems", "alcohol problems", "recovery" (in the context of drug use), and "gender equality". The task becomes considering how specific policy proposals constitute the "problems" they purport to address, with a range of significant effects (see Question 5 in WPR). The next chapter examines those effects described as "subjectification".

CHAPTER 5

Making and Unmaking "subjects"

Abstract This chapter draws on applications of the WPR approach to illustrate the usefulness of reflecting on how policies produce "subjects" through problematization. The argument is made that it is both relevant and important, in terms of policy development, to reflect on the ways in which policies constitute "subjects" as particular kinds of subjects, with possible impact on people's sense of self and behaviors. The chapter shows that, through identifying the "people categories" and the subject positions available in policies, it becomes possible to consider how "subjects" are governed through subjectification effects. Such a form of analysis directs attention to the dividing practices often generated in policies. Further, it shows how specific problem representations produce targeted groups as responsible for an assumed "problem", creating stigma and silencing the operation of other factors.

Keywords subjectification · subject position · dividing practices · stigmatization · governable subjects

The previous chapter illustrated, through examples, the rethinking generated through analyzing governmental problematizations—how "problems" are represented within policies and policy proposals. The remaining chapters in the book explore how governmental problematizations produce, or constitute, "subjects", "objects" and "places". The use of quotation marks, called scare quotes, here, as elsewhere in the book,

C. Bacchi, S. Goodwin, *Poststructural Policy Analysis*,
DOI 10.1057/978-1-137-52546-8_5

signals the poststructural premise that these "things" need to be seen as provisional and in process. Such a perspective creates new openings for change by highlighting the politics—the heterogeneous strategic relations—involved in their "making".

The title of this chapter—making and unmaking "subjects"—refers to the production through policies of *specific kinds of subjects*—e.g., gendered subjects, entrepreneurial subjects, "mad" subjects. This production takes place through the various subject positions—how a "subject" can be thought—made available in policies (see Chapter 3). Coming to "inhabit" a subject position can shape, to an extent, how people think and act. "Subjectification" describes this *making* of "subjects". The term "subject" does not imply stable, extra-discursive choosing subjects who *select* among subject positions. Nor does it mean a predetermined type of person. Rather, provisional "subjects" with multiple selves are produced from plural and contradictory subject positions. Importantly, these "selves" are not *invented* by the subject; they are culturally produced within "meticulous rituals of power" (Dreyfus and Rabinow 1983: 110).

For example, a policy that requires students to repay government loans to fund their higher education once they achieve a certain salary represents the "problem" to be free education. Since, to repay the loan, students assume the subject position of "financial investors in their own economic futures" (Marginson 1997: 225), the policy produces students as entrepreneurial subjects. There is no suggestion in this proposition that students *automatically* develop entrepreneurial subjectivities. However, the continual linking of education to the wherewithal to pay for it *can* "concentrate the minds" of students on financial matters (McPhee 2001). Moreover, through the *practice* of repayment based on salaries the policy produces the subjects it assumes—students who value education in order to improve their prospects of financial gain—rendering them "governable".

As another example, Marsh (2013) describes how representing suicide as a pathological "problem" of "sick" individuals constitutes those who commit suicide as "mad". As with higher education fees "concentrating the minds" of students, this problematization may have implications for how particular people think and act in specific circumstances. As Marsh (2013: 752) argues, the continual linkage of suicide to mental illness "opens up the possibility that those diagnosed as mentally unwell will see the emergence of a desire to die as a natural and inevitable outcome of such illnesses", potentially leading to more suicides. These sorts of implications of governmental problematizations for how people live (and die) are captured in the term "lived effects" (see Chapter 2).

It is important to recognize links between a focus on subjectification and Hacking's (1986) work on "making up people". Hacking offers Davidson's (1990) argument that there were no "perverts" before the latter part of the nineteenth century because perversion, as a disease, and the pervert, as a diseased person, did not exist before that time. Foucault (1990a) makes a similar argument about homosexuals. The suggestion in Foucault's proposal is not that same-sex activities failed to take place earlier in the century but that the label "homosexual" was unavailable for those activities. In these terms "heterosexuals" did not exist either.

The relevance of this insight for policy analysis appears in the heavy reliance in policies, programs and projects on categories of people. Consider these examples: categories based on age, on socio-economic status, on "biology" (male/female, "race"), on ethnicity and on religion. Following Hacking, these categories need to be seen to play a "creative" or productive role, reinforcing forms of identity. For example, the *practice* of ticking the box "female" on numerous administrative forms produces a gendered subject, a "woman". As a result, "people categories" have subjectification effects, making up the "subjects" they appear to describe.

Specific applications of WPR that highlight the effects of "people categories" and subjectification processes within policies form the basis of this chapter. The goal is to illustrate the importance of reflecting on how policies *make up* "subjects" and the potential, where necessary, to reduce deleterious effects through *unmaking* them. The applications have been organized by policy area for convenience, though it is clear in the selections that a WPR analytic strategy aims to emphasize linkages across policy "specialisms" and across international boundaries.

Education Policy

With links to the discussion of higher education "contribution schemes" above, Southgate and Bennett (2014) apply the WPR questions (see WPR Chart on page 20) to higher education policy in Australia and the UK (2008–2013) targeting "non-traditional students". The idea that universities are "exclusive" or "elitist" institutions has come to be regarded as a significant policy "problem" in a number of countries in the past decade. Southgate and Bennett explore how that "problem" is represented through a swathe of policies aimed at "wider participation". They (2014: 25) argue that it is useful to consider how "policy discourses attempt to speak certain types of subjects into being", recognizing that these constitutive processes are not inevitable nor are subjects subservient to them. To this end, they identify two prevalent subject positions within contemporary higher education documents: "the cap(able) student" and "the proper aspirant".

In terms of "the cap(able) student", the authors argue that the proposal that higher education ought to provide opportunities for people *who have the ability* to participate constructs "capability" as an individual attribute that members of under-represented groups are presumed to lack. They (2014: 30) note further how this "meritocratic frame" depends on "pre-entry performance", a particular measure of "cap(ability)". With a specific focus on subjectification effects, Southgate and Bennett (2014: 32) note that, with a notion of cap(ability) as a fixed human attribute, "students may worry: 'what if I don't have the ability?'" and come to have a "lowered opinion of their ability, feel helpless and withdraw (at the very least emotionally) from believing they can achieve".

At the same time, low SES [Socio-Economic Status] students are constituted as lacking in "aspirations". For example, the Bradley *Review of Australian Higher Education* (Bradley et al. 2008: 27) states that: "Barriers to access for such students include their previous educational attainment, no awareness of the long-term benefits of higher education and, thus, no aspiration to participate". Southgate and Bennett (2014: 35–36) describe this formulation of the "'proper' aspirant" as the product of a "neoliberal governmental technology" where populations are made governable through an emphasis on individual self-realization and self-enhancement. They note that, while, for equity practitioners, the "seemingly inclusive logic" of proposals to welcome the capable and increase aspiration is "hard to resist", it remains important to "hold policy to account" by interrogating underlying troubling assumptions such as presumptions about the meaning of "capability" and "aspirations" (Southgate and Bennett 2014: 38).

Bletsas and Michell (2014: 77) develop a similar argument that in the Bradley Review (2008), "low SES students are constructed as inherently lacking in aspirations in current policy discourse and are regarded as 'needier' higher education students in comparison with their higher SES peers". They contrast typical psychological explanations of discrimination with the kind of discursive analysis they offer in which "classism"—normative devaluing of low SES students—is a pervasive cultural logic (Bletsas and Michell 2014: 81). This analytic approach, as the authors describe, side-steps "debates about whether the recommendations made in the Review are the 'right' ones in order to interrogate just what it is that they represent the problem to be" and the potential deleterious implications of that problematization for targeted groups (Bletsas and Michell 2014: 84).

Turning to the area of early childhood education and care (ECEC), the work of Logan et al. (2013) offers insights into the ways in which policies, as techniques of government, create groups and categories of people, with all sorts of implications for how they are treated, what they require and who they are. Their particular focus is how the "installing of a division between children into age categories, over three and under three" in Australia's 1972 *Child Care Act* constituted a critical juncture in the problematization of early childhood education. The *Act*, drawing on child development theory, emphasized the employment of "qualified teachers" primarily for children older than three years of age and the employment of nurses primarily for children younger than three years of age. Such a distinction positioned some ECEC employees as principally providing care and others as principally providing education. The authors contend that this problem representation "narrows ways in which it is possible for teachers to work with children" and "tends to overlook the fundamental role of family, culture and local contexts for children's learning" (Logan et al. 2013: 89). Such an analysis highlights the importance of examining the constitutive dimension of policies: in this case they are shown to make up "children", employees and family and community members as particular types of educational subjects.

Health Policy

The making of "responsibilized subjects"—subjects held to be responsible for their own health and welfare—has been identified as a feature of contemporary neoliberal governmental rationalities (Rose 2000), diverting attention from broad-based social factors that shape lives. Policy analysts using the WPR approach have been able to shed light on how specific policies produce responsibilized subjects and with what effects. In this section, we provide examples from the field of health policy.

Alexander and Coveney (2013) raise important questions about the subjectification effects of contemporary public health recommendations in Canada and Australia to counter the so-called "obesity epidemic" among children. They identify two main proposals in the material they analyzed: first, that physical activity is to be promoted in *all* of the children's activities; and second, that individual responsibility is to be placed on parents/guardians for children's physical activity levels. Underpinning these proposals they identify a kind of Protestant asceticism and a "'less fat equals healthier' discourse" (Alexander and Coveney 2013: 359).

The excessive focus on bodily appearance in the policy texts that the authors study could, in their view, lead to stigma, a demonizing of fat and distorted body image, precipitating eating disorders. The deeply moralizing discourse could also lead to excessive self-surveillance. Meanwhile, specific kinds of parental subjects are "made". Parents are held responsible for the "problem", silencing how specific recommendations are easier for socially and economically advantaged families to follow in terms of financial cost (e.g., sports equipment) or time. As Alexander and Coveney (2013: 357) state: "being an active role model requires that one have time oneself to be physically active". The point of their analysis is not to condemn specific interventions; rather, this form of policy analysis cautions practitioners to reflect on the potentially deleterious implications of proposals that appear to be clearly beneficial and uncontentious.

Henderson and Fuller (2011) express similar concerns about developments in Australian state and national health policy targeting the physical health needs of people with mental health disorders, an issue "problematized" only after 2006. They target two proposals: the shift from specialized mental health services to primary care, involving a fee for service, and the targeting of "unhealthy lifestyle choice" as the primary individual causal factor for poor health outcomes (Henderson and Fuller 2011: 189). The emphasis in health promotion on making "mental health consumers" "active participants in their own physical health care" (New South Wales Department of Health 2009: 8, 10), in their view, promotes neoliberal market rationalities and the "responsibilization" of people with mental health disorders. In addition, such health promotion programs, through targeting "at risk" populations, can be stigmatizing, "resulting in the mentally ill becoming 'multiply stigmatised'" (Henderson and Fuller 2011: 196). In such problem representations, the impact of structural factors, especially access to physical health care, is downplayed. At the same time, governmental sponsorship of service delivery by general practitioners "privileges prevention strategies focused on the individual over strategies that promote the health of the population as a whole" (Henderson and Fuller 2011: 195).

Immigration Policy

Immigration has become an increasingly fraught issue in the last few decades due to the numbers of people trying to escape political persecution, natural disasters or serious deprivation. The United Nations Refugee Agency (UNHCR 2015) reported, in June 2015, that "Globally, one in every 122 humans is either a refugee, internally displaced, or seeking asylum". How these "problems" are represented in policies figures significantly in the lives of these people.

The issue of "irregular migration" in Europe, with tens of thousands of refugees currently (November 2015) moving across the continent, is particularly contentious. With a focus on Scandinavia, Jørgensen (2012) notes that migration becomes a "problem" of "irregularity" through the existence of restrictive immigration laws. With a sharp eye to the specificities in Sweden, Denmark, and Norway, he argues that, in general, "the principles of equity, justice and fairness are sacrificed due to the division between deserving and undeserving groups" (Jørgensen 2012: 59). For example, in Denmark the category "illegal migrant", as opposed to alternatives such as "undocumented" and "paperless", places migrants outside the law as "deviants" and "unentitled". This position creates a tension with human rights commitments, which is resolved by reducing human rights to citizen-based rights and "territorializing" human rights in a way that leads to "state stability" (see Chapter 7).

In all three Scandinavian countries, there is ambiguity surrounding the access of "irregular migrants" to health care with the effect that people so categorized live lives of insecurity, often disappearing "from the authorities to avoid being deported" (Jørgensen 2012: 54). Their labor market position also remains precarious with many employed on an intermittent basis. The European Union's *Sanctions Directive* penalizes employers of irregular migrants (Jørgensen 2012: 60), adding to their vulnerability. In Denmark, the category "assumed departed" makes it possible for the "problem" to be constituted as non-existent. At the same time, there is a "dominant tendency" to present "irregularity" as an individual choice, with such migrants portrayed as "free illegals" or "voluntary sufferers", "through a language focusing on the possibilities of rational and 'voluntary' choice" (Jørgensen 2012: 52). This form of argument resonates with the discussion above of the making of "responsibilized subjects".

Kvist and Peterson (2010) pursue the issue of migrant labor in Europe. Their particular topic is the phenomenon of an increasing sector of domestic (care) work in Sweden and Spain performed predominantly by immigrant women. They note how, in both countries, the primary focus has been on facilitating paid domestic labor in order to increase (non-migrant) women's engagement in the labor force, with the expressed goals of economic growth and gender equality. As a result, the precarious working conditions of domestic workers are overshadowed. The authors emphasize how facilitating the employment of foreign domestic workers makes the current dismantling of the welfare state in these countries more tolerable for "white men and women of the privileged classes", producing them as "governable subjects". Feminist intersectional theory is drawn on to support the need, in analysis of issues such as this one, to question the presumption of a "homogeneous category of women" (Kvist and Peterson 2010: 200).

Economic Policy

Commonly, "the economy" features in policy analysis as a monolithic entity, a kind of "black box" with an independent and distinct identity (see Chapter 3). Borrowed from the field of natural sciences and technology, the term "black box" is a metaphor for devices, systems or situations whose internal workings are hidden, "those things whose contents have become a matter of indifference" (Callon and Latour 1981: 285). Counter this position, poststructural policy analysis draws attention to those "inner workings", highlighting the repeated practices required to enact "the economy". Certain of these practices constitute "subjects" in ways that have deleterious consequences for specific groups of people. Two examples illustrate this dynamic.

On the topic of economic growth, six chapters in a Swedish Report by Vinnova (Anderson et al. 2012), described as "Sweden's innovation agency", use the WPR approach to identify the subject positions made available to women and to men in government policy documents on regional development. A primary question is: "who is constructed as the entrepreneurial citizen capable of promoting innovation?" (Anderson and Berglund 2012: 22). Contributors found that occasionally women and "people with a foreign background" were described as needing to be included if growth is to be achieved. In general, however, women, people with an immigrant background, those who live in small rural regions, and young people are constituted mainly as "lacking" and in need of "special measures". This stigmatized and subordinate subject position is found to discourage active participation, undermining government objectives (Hudson 2012: 86; see also Rönnblom and Keisu 2013).

Goodwin and Voola (2013) examine how the "problem" of microfinance is represented in a key Australian report on the topic (Burkett and Sheehan 2009). In contrast to international linkages between microfinance and poverty alleviation, in Australia the "problem" addressed by microfinance is "most regularly couched in terms of 'financial exclusion'" (Goodwin and Voola 2013: 230). This exclusion is explained predominantly through concepts such as "financial literacy", constituting those excluded as in deficit, i.e., as *lacking* "literacy" (see Chapter 6). Moreover, despite the fact that the bulk of loan applicants and recipients are women, microfinance programs in Australia are generally packaged as gender neutral, rendering invisible the gendered dimensions of both poverty and financial exclusion (Goodwin and Voola 2013: 231).

Transport/Environment Policy

Environmental and transport policies have increased salience due to concerns about climate change and environmental degradation. Studies of the ways in which such policies produce "subjects" of particular kinds provide novel and challenging insights into how pervasive governing knowledges support existing social arrangements. For example, Nielsen and Bonham (2015) use the WPR questions (see WPR Chart on page 20) to critically interrogate a road safety campaign screened by the South Australian Motor Accident Commission (MAC) from 2010 to 2014. As they suggest, such public awareness campaigns provide advice to individuals on how to conduct themselves and hence offer clear proposals for the kind of critical analysis the WPR approach offers. In a televised advertisement, which was part of the campaign, two young men sit awkwardly astride a tandem bicycle, one of them balancing a large "ghetto blaster" on his shoulder. At a stoplight, they eagerly approach a car with two young women in it. They are quickly rebuffed. The young women drive off, the young men cycle slowly through the intersection, exposing the tagline "LOSE YOUR—LICENCE—AND YOU'RE *SCREWED*" (emphasis in original), explaining that they are cycling because they have lost their driving licenses.

The promotional clip conveys the government's policy that unsafe drivers will lose their driving license, constituting "unsafe driving" as the "problem". This problem representation, as elaborated in the advertisement, relies on presuppositions (background knowledges regarding modes of transport, psychological development theories, etc.) that have significant discursive, subjectification, and lived effects. The underlying assumption, that driving a car is both necessary and desirable, relies on an array of knowledges (e.g., evolutionary theories of land-use/transport interactions) that "form the motor vehicle as the most, if not the only, efficient means of transport" (Nielsen and Bonham 2015: 239). "Not driving" is constituted to be a severe social handicap for young men, a form of punishment for presumed unsafe driving practices. The advertisement produces an opposition ("dividing practice") between the unlawful "bad citizen", who has lost his license and must resort to an "inferior" transport option, and the "driver subject", who has maintained their license and assumes the position of the lawful "good citizen" (Nielsen and Bonham 2015: 240). At the same time, the category "youth" is reproduced as a naturalized, "discrete population segment" of risk-takers (Nielsen and Bonham 2015: 237–238).

This normalization of motoring, while unintended, has important implications for how young people may come to scrutinize their behaviors in relation to cycling and driving. Through its negative characterization of cycling, the advertisement also silences the numerous benefits cycling offers to individuals, society, urban liveability and the environment. The important point, as Nielsen and Bonham emphasize, is for policy workers *cum* analysts to reflect critically on the specific "subjects" (cyclists, motorists and young people) and "objects" (cycling, driving, transport; see Chapter 6) constituted in policies, programs, and research (Nielsen and Bonham 2015: 244).

Disability/Equality Policy

Chapter 4 drew upon applications of the WPR approach to query how "gender equality" is problematized within selected ILO and EU policies. These policies linked "gender equality" to employability, producing the "woman worker" as subject position. In her study of how the "problem" of disability is represented in the World Bank's policies of "inclusive development" and "disability mainstreaming" between 2000 and 2011, Marshall (2012a; 2012b) finds some analogous messages for the understanding of disability in development.

To apply the WPR analytic strategy Marshall (2012a: 17) turns to the Bank's website, treating it as a "hypermodal policy text", which incorporates multiple forms of communication (text, images, sound) and electronic linking of text. The website offers advice to organizations on how to deal with disability. It provides a range of proposals that indicate how disability and related terms—such as health, equality, and knowledge—are conceptualized. Specifically, it represents "inclusive development" to be a "problem" of awareness, prevention and social integration.

Relying on assumed knowledges (biomedicine and economics), "inclusive development" constitutes "disability" and "development" as "states of being" (see Chapter 6). It produces two subject positions: a "disabled development subject" and an "ablenormative development subject". The "disabled development subject" is produced as lacking the "skills", education, and training required to perform as a contributing citizen, individualizing the "problem" of exclusion (Marshall 2012a: 269). The goal of "inclusive development" is to make the "disabled development subject" as much like its "ablenormative" counterpart as possible. Disability is constituted as something to be prevented, signaled in the Bank's advancement of the Disability Adjusted Life Year (DALY), which calculates the benefits of health interventions in terms of "disability-free years".

A particular understanding of independence is valorized in this representation of the "problem" of "disability", "closing down consideration of the positive experiences of caring" (Marshall 2012a: 259). Underpinned by an equal opportunity paradigm, the focus is on "removing barriers" to "inclusion", primarily through employment, with productivity essential to "personhood". Such an approach harnesses the poor to the global economy, dehistoricizing the Bank's role in "producing negatively health-impacting situations in developing countries" (Marshall 2012a: 272). In this problem representation there is little space to question the presumed benefits of assimilation to the normative position of development neoliberalism.

Through the privileging of particular forms of knowledge, e.g., technical, "neutral" and "universalistic" (Marshall 2012a: 224), the Bank, dubbed the "Knowledge Bank", constitutes the "subject" of "development professional" as a "technocrat" (Marshall 2012a: 288). However,

Marshall (2012a: 318) postulates that the kind of critical engagement she offers produces a "route" for development policy workers/analysts to "engage in active practices of reflexivity". Thus, her work supports the central argument in the book that, creating the opportunity for policy workers to engage in forms of poststructural analysis, such as WPR, can promote "different types of policy workers who undertake policy work that recognizes the discursive effects of substantive policies on people and social relations" (Gill 2012: 84).

Family Policy

Assumptions about parenting roles were identified as central to understandings of "gender equality" in the preceding chapter. In her study of COPE [Community Parent Education], a Canadian parenting support program offered by Swedish municipalities, Widding (2011: 22) examines the kind of "problem" "poor parenting" is represented to be. The COPE program forms part of Sweden's *National Strategy for Parent Support* aimed at increasing parenting "skills" as a way to respond to concerns about children's deteriorating mental health. It includes a manual and a DVD with twenty-two film sequences. The films are shown to parents in each session. They illustrate what are considered to be poor parenting practices and provide the basis for discussing "right parenting strategies". Hence, parents are produced as responsible for their children's good mental health (Widding 2011: 33).

The manual emphasizes that children need to be taught self-control, as do the parents. Widding (2011: 28) points out that the focus on self-mastery replicates long-standing bourgeois ideals for personal development and success. While social class is not specifically mentioned, this problematizing of lack of restraint resonates with historical child welfare and education interventions aimed at shaping working-class parents according to the "bourgeoisie home and family-oriented ideals" (Widding 2011: 25). Implicitly, therefore, COPE produces working-class patterns of childrearing as problematic. Concerted efforts to recruit migrant parents to the program signal that their parenting practices are also seen to require attention.

In addition, while the *National Strategy* states explicitly that all forms of parent support must reinforce gender equality, the film clips reproduce the conventional role of mother as conciliator and boy children as difficult to discipline. How parenting is represented as a "problem" in these materials, therefore, risks reinforcing prejudices and stereotypes about particular groups and limits "our understanding of other possible ways of parenting in relation to race/ethnicity, social class and gender" (Widding 2011: 30, 36).

The applications of WPR in this chapter illustrate what it means to describe policies as producing, or *making*, "subjects". Poststructural policy analysis, as deployed here, challenges the notion that human beings have unchanging characteristics that policies (simply) "work with"—as assumed in behavioral economics and "nudge" theory[1]. Counter this view, through the ways in which "problems" are represented, policies are involved in shaping what it is possible for "subjects" to become, with important implications for how governing takes place. Such a focus alerts analysts to the possible deleterious subjectification effects of policies and to the dividing practices policies may put in place, prompting policy workers *cum* analysts to "think differently" (Foucault 1986: 8).

Note

1. "Nudging theory" (or "nudge theory") relates to the emerging trend by which governments attempt to modify citizens' behaviors through altering their environments. In this approach, it is assumed that people's behaviors can be anticipated (Haydock 2014).

CHAPTER 6

Making and Unmaking "objects"

Abstract Through applications of the WPR approach from several policy fields, this chapter explores the proposition that policies produce "objects". It draws upon theory introduced in Chapter 3, with emphasis upon the notions of discursive practice, genealogy, and governmentality. The following questions guide the analysis:

- What does it mean to problematize an assumed "object for thought"?
- How are "objects" constituted through governing practices?
- What role do expert knowledges play in constituting "objects for thought"?
- How do concepts become "objects" through measurement?
- How does rethinking "objects" as the products of practices open up space to cultivate alternative problematizations?

Keywords "cycling" · "social inclusion" · "addiction" · "literacy" · "competence" · "wellbeing"

In this chapter, we shift focus from the making of "subjects" to the making of "objects" in governing practices and policy development, understood broadly. Clearly, there are overlaps between the two themes, which have been separated for heuristic purposes. For example, the making of the "mad"

C. Bacchi, S. Goodwin, *Poststructural Policy Analysis*,
DOI 10.1057/978-1-137-52546-8_6

subject, described in Chapter 3, is accompanied by the creation of "madness" as an "object for thought". Moreover, the production of "subjects" as particular kinds of subjects means that, in effect, they are produced, through "modes of objectification" (Foucault 2000: 326), as forms of "object", e.g., as "*a* mother", "*a* welfare recipient", "*an* immigrant".

The "objects" that provide the targets of analysis for this chapter consist of concepts and categories that play a prominent role in governing practices. Here we adopt Lakoff's (1987) position that, to call something a "tree" or to say something has "merit" is, in both instances, to make a case that the things so labeled have characteristics in common and hence form a category. To challenge the status of categories as "objects" does not mean bringing their existence into question; rather, it means challenging their existence as *fixed* (Chia 1996: 32–33). As with "subjects" in Chapter 5, such "things" are conceived to be in ongoing formation, and attention is directed to the heterogeneous practices involved in their making. To illustrate what this means we include "hard-edged" categories such as "traffic" and "cycling", and a broad sweep of more amorphous conceptual categories that feature prominently in policy development ("poverty", "social inclusion", "addiction", "literacy", "competence", "wellbeing", "disability", "development").

Concerning the latter group, there is a long tradition of engagement with the importance of the contested meanings ascribed to political concepts (Bacchi 1996: 1). As an obvious example, the concept "equality" often evokes debates about whether it refers to "equality of opportunity" or "equality of outcome" (Hoffman and Graham 2006). There is also extensive literature on the significance of interpreting "health" to mean (simply) the absence of disease or as imparting some more holistic notion of "wellbeing", a concept that is itself contested (Wright and McLeod 2015; see below). As Tanesini (1994: 207) points out, concepts are not descriptive of anything; rather, they are "proposals about how we ought to proceed from here". As proposals, they are problematizations, open to interrogation (see Chapter 2).

In many, if not in most cases, however, concepts come to assume a certain taken-for-granted facticity or entitative status—something that has a real existence—in policy development and policy analysis. They come to be spoken of as "objects", closed to critical scrutiny. This tendency reflects the trend among users of the English language to "focus more on categories and classifications which define a thing and fix its nature for all time" with less concern for "processes, movement and change"

(Hoagland 1988: 224). A poststructural approach to concepts and categories *returns* attention to those processes, movement, and change. In a poststructural account "objects" do not exist as essences; they emerge as "objects for thought" in practices. As Veyne (1997: 160–161; emphasis in original) describes: "*What is made*, the object, is explained by what went into its *making* at each moment of history; we are wrong to imagine that the *making*, the practice, is explained on the basis of what is made".

In this poststructural perspective, recalling the role of vocabulary as a political technology (see Chapter 3), categories and concepts are "denaturalized, made specific and their governmental implications revealed" (Larner 2008: 23). The goal becomes making the criteria that define an "object" more noticeable. What goes into its making? Which practices require repetition on a regular basis for it to be produced? And, what effects accompany its production and use? Through this analysis, the politics—the heterogeneous strategic relations—involved in constituting what is "real" become visible.

The applications of WPR in this chapter illustrate the "objectivization" of categories and concepts that figure prominently in the constitution of policy "problems", and hence are important exemplars for those who develop and analyze policy. They tread the uneasy line between challenging the "transhistorical reality of natural objects" and granting "those objects enough objective reality so that they remain something to be explained" (Veyne 1997: 169 fn 7). Through examining the processes involved in the formation of concepts and categories as "objects" and through reflecting on the effects that follow from the problem representations they enable, these contributions support the proposition that it is timely for policy workers/analysts to place "contested *objects*" alongside "contested *concepts*"!

"TRAFFIC"/"CYCLING"

What does it mean to call a "thing's" entitative status into question? Veyne's (1997: 160) explanation, provided in Chapter 3, is that: "[T]here are no natural objects.... There are only multiple objectivizations ('population', 'fauna', 'subjects under law'), correlatives of heterogeneous practices". As a result, the analytical emphasis shifts from presumed "objects" to the relations involved in their "becoming". To illustrate this proposition, we draw on Nielsen and Bonham's (2015; see also Bonham et al. 2015) work on problematizations in the fields of transport and environmental policy (introduced in Chapter 5) to trouble the taken-for-granted "objects" of "traffic" and "cycling". Through identifying the discursive practices involved in the emergence of these categories, Nielsen and Bonham defamiliarize and politicize them.

As explained in Chapter 3, a discursive practice refers to the network of practices and relations involved in producing "knowledge" and "*what* is said". It involves "a historically specific set of routines through which social knowledges are continually formed" (Bonham et al. 2015: 181; Bacchi and Bonham 2014). A study of discursive practices, therefore, directs attention away from assumed fixed categories of thought ("objects") to the relations involved in their production, helping to make noticeable the criteria that define them. For example, Foucault explains how "madness" emerged as an "object for thought" in the practices of exclusion and internment of those called "mad" (see "Practices, Events, Relations" in Chapter 3).

Turning to "traffic" Nielsen and Bonham describe the plethora of relations which operated, in the early-to-mid-twentieth century, to "forge 'traffic' as an object for thought out of a multitude of street activities":

> interactions between people in public space; materials such as road surfaces and hawkers' carts; behaviours like standing about, or alighting from a tram; parliamentary speeches about gambling in the street; engineering discussions regarding the weight of vehicles; regulations relating to loitering and furious driving; newspaper reports on "hit and run" fatalities; contestations over how to conduct oneself in public.... (Nielsen and Bonham 2015: 234; see also Bonham 2006)

How the "problem" of "traffic" is constituted relies on the knowledges produced in these practices. Key sites (community, parliament, law courts, media) in this network of relations participated, albeit with different levels of authority, in the production of "traffic" as a self-evident "object". This *naturalization* of "traffic" has important implications for "urban" planning, street design, industry policy, and so on (Nielsen and Bonham 2015: 234).

"Cycling" and "bicycles" are also "objects" in *ongoing formation* (Bonham et al. 2015). Alongside the "cycling subject", described in Chapter 5, "cycling" is produced through a wide range of practices, involving materials, movements, documents, words, symbols, and so forth. Amongst those practices, Nielsen and Bonham (2015) include the advertisements designed by the Motor Accident Commission to warn of the possible dire social consequences of losing one's license—being compelled to cycle!—producing "cycling" as an inferior mode of transport.

"Traffic" and "cycling", however, do not describe fixed entities. They are formed within a multiplicity of discursive practices, including transport, road safety, psychology, and economic and national development, and hence can be re-formed. Some of these discursive practices, for example, health and environment, produce "traffic" as problematic and "cycling" as a valuable way of traveling. Within each site (see above) activity is involved; decisions are made about which "elements" to assemble together (although there is no assumption of intentional manipulation). Such a perspective prompts policy workers *cum* analysts to reflect upon the "realities" their decisions create and to consider which "objects" are affirmed and rendered "fact" in the day-to-day practices of developing policies. The perspective outlined here emphasizes the activity involved in the production of "objects", opening a space for them to be produced otherwise through alternative practices.

"POVERTY"/"SOCIAL INCLUSION"

Much political debate has occurred historically over how "poverty", a term ubiquitous in social policy, is to be defined and understood (Bletsas 2012). For example, the so-called "agency/structure" debate pits those who tend to portray "poverty" as due to the personal failings of "the poor" against those who emphasize structural inequalities. How does a poststructural account contribute to a rethinking of these issues?

As Bletsas (2012: 40) explains, poststructuralism does not put the "reality" of poverty, "understood as the experience of extreme disadvantage and deprivation", into question. Rather, it challenges the notion that "poverty" has some sort of existence independent of the policies that "address" it. Drawing on governmentality theory (see "Governmentality: Rationalities and Technologies" in Chapter 3), an emphasis is placed on the ways in which particular governmental rationalities—e.g., social democratic, liberal, neoliberal, etc.—*problematize* "poverty", in effect producing different "poverties". In this account, "poverty" (like "traffic" and "cycling") is always being actively produced and the task becomes teasing out the implications, or effects (see Question 5 in WPR Chart on page 20), that arise when "poverty" is constituted as a particular kind of problem.

For example, Bletsas (2012: 46) describes how Australian Compulsory Income Management policy (see Chapter 3) produces "poverty" as something restricted to specific communities, those deemed to be incapable of managing their own income. Hence, the policy constitutes "poverty" as a residual "problem" and the "product of internal dysfunction" rather than as a consequence of broad-based social relationships. As another example, Bletsas points to the way in which the Australian Government's response to a Senate Committee Report on Poverty, entitled *A Hand Up Not a Hand Out*, constitutes the "problem" of poverty. The response reads:

> The Government has a strong record on and commitment to improving the well-being of all Australians and to addressing social disadvantage by assisting and supporting people in establishing *their own* goals, making *their choices, accepting responsibility* and *taking advantage of opportunities* (Australian Commonwealth Government 2005: 5, in Bletsas 2007: 70; emphasis added by Bletsas).

As Bletsas (2007: 70) describes, "The focus on individual choices, goals and responsibilities shifts attention away from any particular policy area and on to individual behaviours as causing the 'problem'".

Turning to "social inclusion", an umbrella term in the UK and Australia for issues relating to "poverty", Bletsas (2007: 74) notes how, tacitly, the three priority areas targeted for intervention by South Australia's Social Inclusion Unit (SIU)—homelessness, drug use, and school retention—"focus on individuals who exhibit certain behaviours as the locus of the problematic social exclusion(s)". On homelessness, more attention is paid to "triggers", such as "relationship breakdown" and "eviction", than to economic and social factors. On drug use, a heavy endorsement of the need for young people to develop "resilience" produces "drug dependence" as a "project of individual will". On school retention, SIU proposals produced a "failure" to "connect" with the "formalised apparatus of education" as the "problem", silencing possible inadequacies within the education system (Bletsas 2007: 75–78). A range of other applications of WPR (Edwards 2010; Marshall 2012a; Pereira 2014) similarly highlights the individualizing and integrationist character of specific "social inclusion" policies.

Lest this analysis look like a recreation of the agency/structure dichotomy (see above), Bletsas (2012: 43) points out that the agency/structure debate is itself "a product of western forms of sociological and philosophical thought", rather than a product of something inherent in "poverty". To move past this dilemma, a focus on "poverty" as problematization encourages critical engagement with the *precise* ways in which "poverty" is constituted in *specific* policies, how it is created as a particular kind of "object" within identified problematizations, and with what implications for those governed through these problematizations.

"ADDICTION"

The concept "addiction" forms an "object" in many policy fields, most obviously in health policy. Disputes over its meaning have a long history. For some time sociologists have drawn attention to the cultural construction of the concept (Room 1983; Gusfield 1996). A poststructural approach moves beyond social constructionism to focus on the practices involved in the production of "addiction" as a particular kind of condition or disease in specific contexts. A prominent place is assigned to the role of governmental practices and technologies in this production, with "governmental" encompassing professional and expert knowledges (see "Governmentality: Rationalities and Technologies" in Chapter 3).

One such governmental technology, the *Diagnostic and Statistical Manual of Mental Disorders* (*DSM*), which is based on psychological "knowledge", is central to the production of "addiction". Drawing upon Science and Technology Studies (STS), Keane et al. (2011: 876) explain the point: "all diagnostic instruments and practices construct their objects rather than describe a pre-existing 'reality'", making the *DSM* an "actant" in "ontological politics" (see Mol 1999, and Chapter 1). Indeed, the *DSM* has reviewed its criteria for "addiction" and related terminology on several occasions (Fraser 2013: 501). The most recent incarnation, *DSM-5*, returns the term "addictive" to the description of "substance-related disorders". It also includes "gambling disorder as the sole condition in a new category on behavioral addictions" (American Psychiatric Association 2013). In each case, supported by developments in neuroscience, which proposes the "brain disease" model of "addiction", the individual becomes the locus of the "problem".

The addition of gambling to the "addiction" lexicon signals the growing proliferation of "addictions" in contemporary scientific analysis. There are now references to sex, shopping, and eating *addictions* (Fraser 2013), alongside "internet use". As Fraser et al. (2014: 235) suggest, this trend toward "addict*ing*"—seeing more and more activities in terms of "addiction"[1]—has important political implications, pathologizing ever larger numbers of people and individualizing complex social issues. It also signals the volatility of the term "addiction" and indicates the "work" (or activity) involved in its production. A key analytic task becomes ensuring that such "work" is "noticed" and brought under scrutiny (see Law 2004).

To this end Fraser and Moore (2011: 499) turn to poststructural methods of policy analysis, including WPR, to examine "how the problem of ATS [Amphetamine-Type Stimulants] use has been formulated in policy" in Australia. They analyze the "textual strategies" around causation and evidence involved in key policy documents to illustrate how specific "recommendations and measures presented as following from the problem of ATS use" are authorized.

In another application, Moore and Fraser (2013: 921) show how the funding and reporting processes required by a specific treatment system for "addiction"—the "episode-of-care" system—in Victoria, Australia, produces the "problem" it assumes. To maintain funding through achieving "significant treatment goals", "episodes" are closed off after four or five sessions, and new ones opened, sometimes for the same service user. This "bureaucratization of disease" (Rosenberg 2003) transforms the complex experiences of, and interactions between, alcohol and other drug workers and service users into "measurable units" to facilitate "performance measurement". In the process, "addiction" is produced as a "discrete, bounded entity amenable to treatment in episodic fashion". Among the many deleterious implications canvassed (Moore and Fraser 2013), the focus on the "countable number of addicts" creates the impression that the "problem" of "addiction" is escalating. This example of "objectivization" well illustrates how poststructural policy analysis brings attention to the constitutive effects of policy practices.

"LITERACY"

Like "addiction", "literacy" is currently enjoying something of an expansion in relation to policy development. Alongside references to "benchmarks" on "literacy and numeracy" among school students, there are allusions to "financial literacy" (Bastian and Coveney 2013: 165), "health literacy" (Green et al. 2015) and, in Australia, "Asia literacy" (Salter 2013), each attracting controversy and debate. These new adaptations of the term signal both its mutability and its political relevance. And yet "literacy" is most often presented as an abstract entity, "something that can be quantified and measured across whole sections of population" (Kelly 2015: 273). The applications in this subsection of the chapter withstand such "*a priori* concept definitions" (Hansen 2014). Instead, they depict "literacy" as a process and a governmental technology that contributes to the production of "governable subjects" (Chapter 5) and "governable places" (Chapter 7).

Adopting a Foucauldian genealogical approach Kelly (2015) positions "literacy" policy in Australia within a "security apparatus", broadly understood to encompass national prerogatives regarding the constitution of population and economic concerns. Such associations are illustrated in the White Australia Policy, a restrictive approach to immigration from Federation in 1901 to the latter part of the twentieth century, in which "the literacy test was the instrument of whiteness par excellence" (Lake 2006: 229). More recent (post-2007) national citizenship tests use English language proficiency to determine the inclusion/exclusion of possible "citizens", instituting a dividing practice.

Developments in Australia reflect the international context, indicated in the influence of studies by the Organization for Economic Cooperation and Development (OECD). For example, the *Programme for International Student Assessment* (PISA), which tabulates and compares national literacy proficiency indicators in the areas of reading, numeracy, and science, produces "literacy" as "one measure of human outputs and by implication national productivity" (Kelly 2015: 21). Such measurement exercises illustrate how governing takes place through numbers and comparison (see "Governmentality: Rationalities and Technologies" in Chapter 3), in this instance firming up the "object" status of "literacy".

In Norway, as Mausethagen (2013) describes, the term "competence" has come to be preferred to "literacy". She draws upon the thinking within a WPR analytic strategy to investigate the ways in which policy texts represent the "problem" of "competence". Her particular target is a 2004 White Paper, *Culture for Learning*, (Ministry of Education and Research 2004: 30–31), which endorsed the definition of "competence" put forward by the OECD[2] as "the ability to meet complex challenges". Such an understanding, suggests Mausethagen (2013: 170), shifts the emphasis in education from "factual knowledge" to students' ability to adapt to a changing employment environment. The same White Paper holds teachers accountable for demonstrating "competencies", assessed on the basis of "increased student outcomes". Mausethagen (2013: 176) expresses concern that evaluating teacher performance through a system of sanctions or incentives for results has possible "adverse side effects in terms of equity and social inclusion". For students and teachers, she argues, "competence" is produced as a "problem" of individual abilities, performance and "outputs", reflecting a neoliberal rationality.

Along related lines Salter (2013) explores the implications of a relatively new conceptual "object" in Australia, "Asia literacy"—the professed need for students to become "literate" about Asia. Salter notes that the "solution" of "Asia literacy" produces the "problem" of Australian education as framed primarily by economic concerns. Usefully, Salter (2013: 5) draws on Bhabha's (1984) notion of mimicry to read policy texts against themselves, enabling the identification of "marginalised concerns" and the development of alternatives to dominant frameworks.

Together, these studies illustrate that "literacy" is always being produced as a particular kind of "object"—or replaced by an equally contested "object", e.g., "competence"—and that policy plays a central role in the production process. While the term "literacy" may sound benign and indeed worthwhile, it is important to reflect on what goes into its making and with what effects.

States of Being: "wellbeing", "disability", "developing/developed"

"States of being" function as particularly powerful "objects for thought" in policy development. "Wellbeing", for example, operates as a keyword in contemporary policy deliberations, both internationally and in specific countries (e.g., UK, Australia). While there is much debate in the scholarly literature about its precise meaning, it tends to be used with assurance in numerous policy debates and documents.

The proliferation of "wellbeing" indices helps to explain its "objectivization". The OECD (2013) *Better Life Initiative* produces regular reports on "wellbeing" in different countries. UNICEF (2013) also produces "league tables" on child wellbeing. When some "thing" is counted in these ways, it achieves status as a kind of entity. Its collective character is also promoted. For example, a recent headline in a major Australian newspaper reads: "Key measure of *Australia's* wellbeing has been stagnant for two years" (Wade 2015; emphasis added).

McLeod and Wright (2015: 5) challenge the assumed "object" status of "wellbeing". They show that the concept in effect constitutes a form of proposal and hence operates as a problematization. That is, the concept contains a diagnosis of a "problem"—lack of wellbeing—directing attention to the specific policy initiatives designed to "address" that apparent lack. Through interrogating the assumptions underpinning representations of the "problem" in those initiatives and considering what is left unproblematic, it becomes possible to think of the "problem" differently. In tune with observations in this chapter regarding current iterations of "social inclusion", "addiction", and "literacy", McLeod and Wright (2015: 3) observe, both in the UK and in Australia, a shift in wellbeing discourses from a broad concern with "the body politic" to an overriding emphasis on "the body personal"—"wellbeing that is actively produced by the choosing consumer". This emphasis is associated with a neoliberal rationality.

McLeod and Wright are particularly concerned with the frequent connections drawn between "youth" and "wellbeing". They note how the prefix "youth" gives a particular urgency to "wellbeing": "[T]hese discussions are commonly framed by a sense of alarm and grave concerns about how young people are faring" (McLeod and Wright 2015: 2). Their analysis endorses but moves beyond the view that "youth" is a socially constructed concept to consider how "youth wellbeing" functions in policy formulation—"what it does, where it goes, what it opens up and shuts down, and what it makes possible and impossible to think and to do" (McLeod and Wright 2015: 5). This approach illustrates the importance of reflecting on the constitutive effects that accompany specific problem representations, and the usefulness of the WPR framework as a means to do so[3].

Marshall (2012a) explores the "objectivization" of "disability" and "developing/developed" as states of being in her WPR analysis of World Bank policies (see Chapter 5). She highlights the role played by expert knowledges (e.g., medicine and economics) in producing these categories as presumed fixed essences. Even among advocates of a broad social interpretation of "health" she finds a "foundational ontological conceptualization of the body as a 'pre-given', natural object" (Marshall 2012a: 182), and hence, the production of "disability" as a naturalized condition. Such a view makes it difficult to discern (and critique) the practices, including the policy practices (Fulcher 1989), involved in *making* "disability". For example, McEwan and Butler (2007: 463) note that "what is striking about much international debate is a failure to recognise 'development' itself as potentially disabling", a theme pursued in the next chapter.

The kind of thinking promoted in this chapter can be simultaneously inspiring and confronting. It illustrates how policy analysts use WPR to subject "objects for thought", often associated with popular reform initiatives (e.g., "social inclusion", "literacy", "wellbeing"), to critical interrogation—asking how they have been practiced into existence and with what effects. While some may find it disconcerting to so scrutinize concepts and categories commonly adopted in their work, this process of defamiliarization makes it possible to reflect on the limitations and possible deleterious consequences of well-established frameworks of meaning and the conceivable need for alternative problematizations. In this way, space is opened up to think differently.

Notes

1. In this usage Fraser et al. (2014) adopt the poststructural convention of "gerunding", using verb forms instead of nouns, to highlight how "things" are made to be and are in constant formation. See "Power, Knowledge, and Resistance" in Chapter 3; see also Bacchi and Eveline (2010) on "gendering".
2. The definition is in line with the OECD-project DeSeCo, *Definition and Selection of Key Competencies.*
3. McLeod and Wright (2015: 6) note that the chapters in *Rethinking Youth Wellbeing* (Wright and McLeod, 2015) "offer the kinds of interrogation called for by Bacchi".

CHAPTER 7

Making and Unmaking "places"

Abstract The challenge in this chapter is to rethink commonly assumed geographical "entities" or "places". Such "entities" play a pivotal role in how governing takes place and are most often treated by policy makers as taken-for-granted physical sites or locations. The chapter shows how poststructural policy analysis, illustrated in applications of WPR, encourages policy workers/analysts to consider "places" as political creations. Specifically, it illustrates how, through the lens of problematization and a focus on practices, it becomes possible to interrogate the underlying precepts and assumptions that are necessary to the constitution of named "places". The following questions guide the account:

- What does it mean to challenge the existence of "places" as fixed and stable "entities"?
- What is accomplished through this form of analysis?
- What strategies are available to problematize named "places"?
- What are the implications of a poststructural perspective for research on assumed "places", such as "nation-states", "cities", and "public places"?

Keywords "the state" · "Europe" · "urban/rural" · "developed/developing" · "public places"

C. Bacchi, S. Goodwin, *Poststructural Policy Analysis*,
DOI 10.1057/978-1-137-52546-8_7

This chapter illustrates that—as with other types of "objects"—nations, regions, zones, and so on, are "objectivized" (Veyne 1997: 160), that is, turned into "objects", through policies. Following the analytic strategy adopted in Chapter 6, therefore, attention shifts from assumed "objects" to the practices, including the governmental techniques, involved in their production. For example, below we examine briefly the function of signposts and other "inscriptions" (Walters 2002a) in making (up) "Europe", the role of statistics in generating "urban/rural" and "developing/developed" "places", and the role of monitoring and surveillance policies in making (up) "public places".

In conventional policy analysis, the geographic or spatial elements of policy are largely taken for granted or treated as self-evident. "Place" is usually considered fixed and non-contestable. "Places" appear as context, or backdrop, for the other changes, challenges, and contestations that occur. At the same time, the designation of "places" plays a critical role in how governing occurs. Consider not simply the more abstract notions of "nation" or "the state", but also the more precise specification of "planning zones" and "public places". This stance, indicative of many social science studies, makes it "sensible" to ask questions about *a country's* foreign policy or *a city's* infrastructure policy, as if these "places" are natural, unified, and stable locales.

Walters (2009: 495) cautions against this tendency to ontologize our spatial concepts. He asks: what is a region? a zone? a territory? a network? an area? and, with Larner, suggests that policy analysts need to become "much more nominalistic about the diversity of global spaces" (Larner and Walters 2004: 16). In nominalism the terms used (e.g., "state", "urban") are simply the names assigned to "things". The point here is to consider how complex political spatial relations come to be described through terms such as "state", "urban", "Europe", and so on, and to reflect critically on the effects accompanying such labeling. There is a need to ask, for example—what follows from constituting economic relations in terms of "special economic zones"?

The habit of treating "place" as context *for* policies, rather than as produced, reproduced and transformed *by* policies, can be traced to the notion of government as consisting only of conventional legislative institutions and state-generated rules, regulations, provisions, and punishments. In this view, policies are understood as predominantly activities of state institutions, operating in defined territories—or jurisdictions—where they have achieved sovereign power. Fenna (2004: 5), for example, describes public policies as involving "an exercise of the sovereign power of government", which can be "backed by legitimate force" in "any particular country or jurisdiction". These "places"—"jurisdictions"—are represented as territories with fixed borders and legitimated rulers, and are made singular and homogenized by designating populations as *citizens* of that *jurisdiction*.

From a governmentality perspective (see Chapter 3), this understanding of policy restricts analysis to the institutions or political power of "the state", narrowly conceived, and neglects other ways in which governing takes place. It also depoliticizes the "where" and "how" of policy. In a kind of circular logic, governments are seen as legitimate in their responsibility for governing territories—"places"—(simply) because they govern them. The work, or activity, that goes into shaping territories and populations in specific, sometimes contentious ways, so that governing *can take place* is disregarded. By contrast, poststructural policy analysis suggests that we see "the state" as the "outcome of political activities as well as a contribution to them" (Finlayson and Martin 2006: 155) and scrutinize critically the various practices that are "necessary to create territories out of contingent and ambiguous lands and peoples" (Kuehls 1996: xii).

To achieve this goal and thus to understand how "nations" and other geographical "entities" *come to be*, attention is directed to the technologies involved in their production and the rationalities underpinning those technologies. The emphasis shifts from conventional political institutions to the networks of relations among various agencies and experts involved with "the state" in making "territories" and populations governable—which Foucault (1991c) describes as the *governmentalization* of the state. As subsequent analyses in this chapter illustrate, a study of problematizations, facilitated through asking the WPR questions (see WPR Chart on page 20), opens up this field of relations and practices to critical analysis, making it possible to reconsider how space is currently organized.

MAKING (UP) "THE STATE"

A good deal of discussion about public policy assumes the existence of a body or "place" called "the state", although it is usually imagined more in terms of jurisdiction than physical location. We have already signaled disquiet with equating "nation-state" status and sovereign rule, a theme vigorously pursued by poststructural international relations and feminist scholars (Ashley 1988; Pringle and Watson 1992; Walker 1993). In tune with these critiques, this section offers a rethinking of "the state" as a space of shifting relations and practices, making it possible to debate inclusions and exclusions, undertakings and refusals.

In an important article on "The subject and power", Foucault (2000) explains that, while power relations are not restricted to "the state", historically, they have come to be more and more under state control (see Chapter 3). That is, "all other forms of power must refer to it", even if they are not reducible to the form of "the state".

> Using here the restricted meaning of the word "government", one could say that power relations have been progressively governmentalized, that is to say, elaborated, rationalized and centralized in the form of, or under the auspices of, state institutions. (Foucault 2000: 345)

Instead of treating "the state" as some sort of closed and timeless "entity", therefore, the task becomes seeking out and exploring the shifting constitution of "state" power in particular times and places. To accomplish this analysis, Foucault recommended the study of problematizations.

As an illustration, Kelly (2015) explores how "literacy" has become a "problem" of "state" security in Australia. Specifically, his analysis of government policy and key policy speeches on education from Federation in 1901 to 2007 reveals how the *parameters of "the state"* come to encompass concern and control around the ability to speak and write English. To contextualize this study, Kelly produces a genealogy of a "security-development nexus" at the end of the Cold War, emphasizing the formative influence of United Nations deliberations (see below). In this mode of analysis, the "black box" of "the state" is opened up to examine how the boundaries of state activities involve continual definition and redefinition of what is within the competence of "the state" and what is not. The effects of such redefinition are also highlighted. For example, as Kelly (2015: 259–260) notes, a "state" focus on literacy "as a measurable and culturally normative activity" has the capacity to exclude, as in the case of remote Indigenous communities and prospective immigrants.

Making (up) "Europe"

This section opens up another "black box"—"Europe"—though the questions it raises could be asked in relation to any "nation-state" or pan-national entity (e.g., "Asia"). "Europe", however, provides a useful example to demonstrate a poststructural and governmentality perspective because of its longstanding, historical associations (e.g., as a continent, or even as a civilization). Within the last few decades, "Europe" has become more "positive", in the sense that its meaning and place in the world of geopolitics has been *firmed up*. It has become a "domain of statistics, calculation and projections—the object and the subject of a whole range of policies" (Walters in Tietäväinen et al. 2008: 67). How has this happened?

The perspective offered in this book challenges any suggestion that this development *had to* happen, that there is a logical and necessary evolution in the formation of territorial states. Far from being timeless, they are understood to be "the product of institutional dynamics, social constructions, political and geopolitical struggles, and economic forces" (Walters 2009: 488). To understand the "objectivization" of "Europe", therefore, attention is directed to the precise "practices, technologies or techniques that made it possible at a certain time for an organization to govern key dimensions of social and economic life in the name of Europe" (Walters in Tietäväinen et al. 2008: 67)—which Foucault calls "the arts of government" (Gordon 1991: 3). This pluralization of the "factors" producing "places", such as "Europe", usefully opens up possibilities for change, should change be deemed either appropriate or necessary.

For "Europe" to become a "place", "it" had (and has) to be known. And, to become the kind of "place" it is, as we experience it today, it had (and has) to be known in certain ways. Technologies and policies, the knowledges upon which both rely, and the authoritative knowledges they generate, provide the mechanisms for such knowing to occur. The forms of reason, or rationalities that underpin those technologies and knowledges shape "Europe" as a particular kind of "place". To gain access to underlying rationalities—and so to understand the kind of "place" "Europe" has become (is becoming)—requires examining how technologies, including policies, problematize issues.

For example, Walters (2002a) explores how the apparently innocuous policy affecting signposts at airports serves to designate and firm up both "Europe" as a "place" and the category of "the European". As part of the *Schengen acquis*, which establishes principles for cooperation among "European member states", different checkpoints are established for specific groups—one for "persons covered by Community law" and one for "third-country nationals" (Council of the European Union 1999, in Walters 2002a: 107). The expressed purpose, "speeding up controls" for the first group of people, is facilitated through the passport control signs of "EU" [European Union], in a circle surrounded by stars, and "Non-EU Nationals", directing passengers into different queues.

The significance of these signposts lies far beyond their purely technical and administrative function. For example, by problematizing speed of transit, they invoke an economic rationality of efficiency.[1] In addition, the assumption of territorialized citizenship constitutes a dividing practice at the level of human population (Hindess 2000). Moreover, the reliance on a broad array of knowledges and professionals (e.g., graphic designers, security "experts", IT specialists) illustrates the heterogeneous and pervasive character of governing practices. Inscriptions, including signposts, maps (Gugerli 1998), memoranda, reporting forms, charts, and so on, form part of the numerous "mundane features of rule" that constitute "Europe" as a "knowable, regulatable space" (Walters 2002a: 84). They help to "objectify" "Europe" and to render the governing of "Europe" practical (Walters 2002a: 108; Walters in Tietäväinen et al. 2008: 67).

In this form of analysis, there is a shift in focus from the study of (existing) borders to the practices of border*ing*—another example of the poststructural convention of gerunding (see Chapters 3 and 6). Such a shift highlights the ongoing activity involved in generating "places" (van Houtum 2005).[2] "Borders" emerge as technologies of power, which contribute to the "production of population as a knowable, governable entity" (Walters 2002b: 573). For example, Walters (2002b: 575) describes how the Schengen border is "no longer reducible to fixed control posts and sites of inspection and observation". Instead, it is "networked, an articulation of social security and health data systems, employment registers", "making entry quick and efficient for some, and difficult for others". Importantly, there is no assumption of a linear path of progression or of inevitability in these developments; rather, there are contingent "borders" and contingent "places", prompting analysis and critique.

Making (up) "urban"/"rural" "places"

Extensive literatures in geopolitics and urban studies (see MacLeod and Jones 2011) engage with questions about the nature of "the urban" and the constitution of "cities". Several WPR applications illustrate how policies, in specific contexts, produce an "urban/rural" dichotomy, with implications for food production (Wiseman 2012), climate change

(Holmgren 2015), the treatment of Indigenous peoples (Goodwin 2011), and gender relations (Rönnblom and Sandberg 2015).

Wiseman (2012) analyses how food production is problematized in a key strategy document on primary industries and regions in South Australia (Government of South Australia 2012). Applying WPR questions (see WPR Chart on page 20), he finds that "food" is produced as an economic and industrial "object", and "food production" is an "industry". Since zoning laws designate "the urban" as a *non-industrial* site, it follows that there is no conceptual space for "food" production *within* "urban" regions.

As Wiseman (2012: 30) describes, economic "experts" and a wide range of calculative and measuring techniques, including a multitude of annual statistical surveys on production data and "performance", help to *make up* "the urban" as a "place" where "food" is *not* produced, and peri-urban locales as "places" where production is limited or curtailed. These practices are silenced or rendered invisible in the constitution of "urban" and "rural" as separate economic and social spheres. Additional silences include:

> the myriad social and environmental effects that the "food industry" has helped create, including the displacement and impoverishment of third world peasant farmers, depopulation and decline of first world rural communities and family farms, environmental pollution (top soil loss, water eutrophication, GM contamination, climate change, etc.). (Wiseman 2012: 28–29)

Given the poststructural premise that "objects" are in ongoing formation and subject to change, Wiseman considers the potential of the notion of "food sovereignty", which problematizes "food" as an object of "rights", "justice", and "solidarity", to disrupt and re-make global and local food production arrangements (Wiseman 2012: 37).

Paralleling Wiseman's analysis, Holmgren (2015: 27) shows how contemporary Swedish forestry policy constitutes "forests" as economic objects or, in her words, as "production objects". This development has to be understood in the context of the UNFCCC (United Nations Framework Convention on Climate Change), which endorses "terrestrial carbon sequestration" and forests as "carbon sinks". As a result, wood use in construction (as opposed to reducing emissions) becomes a viable carbon mitigation strategy, and climate change moves "from being a threat to becoming a business opportunity" (Holmgren 2015: 68; see also Holmgren and Arora-Jonsson 2015). This policy produces an "urban/rural" dichotomy, which supports intensive management of forests in countries such as Sweden and conservation of tropical forests in so-called "developing countries" (Holmgren 2015: 67; see below).

As Holmgren (2015: 67) argues, this representation of the "problem" implicitly privileges "the urban" and fails to put in question the interdependencies *between* "rural" and "urban" spaces. For example, it neglects the ways in which consumption in urbanized populations induces intensive commercial food production in rural landscapes, increasing the pressure on tropical forests. Additional silences include the displacement of other forest uses (e.g., common pastures, firewood supply) and the impact on Indigenous populations (i.e., the Sámi).

Goodwin (2011) considers how, in 2007, in Australia, the Northern Territory Emergency Response (NTER) —a set of wide-ranging policies framed as a national response to child sexual abuse in Indigenous communities—produced a new territorial "object", referred to as "prescribed communities". This "object" was constituted through special provisions that singled out "non-urban" Aboriginal people in particular ways. For example, due to the suspension of the *Racial Discrimination Act 1975 (Cth)* within these designated communities, their members could be treated differently from other Australians on the grounds of race, without fear of a legal challenge (Partridge 2014: 16). Thus, "prescribed communities" are constituted as "other" to mainstream Australia. In addition, as Goodwin (2011: 176) suggests, alongside a new geographical "object" to be governed—"prescribed communities"—the legislation *produces* a new policy "subject", the "non-urban" Aboriginal person, who is attributed responsibility for the "problem" of child sexual abuse.

Rönnblom and Sandberg (2015) raise critical questions about several urban development projects aimed at producing Umeå, Sweden's largest northern city, as a "more gender equal" place. Building on Massey (1994; 2005) and in line with the poststructural perspective developed in this chapter, they describe "place" as "flexible", and the "gender-equal city" as *made* in a continuous process, "constructed through power relations, where power is understood as relational and productive" (Rönnblom and Sandberg 2015: 3; see Chapter 3).

Within the projects they study, Rönnblom and Sandberg (2015: 9) identify three "imaginaries", which problematize "gender (in)equality" in different ways: one which *articulates* and thus (simply) "brands" Umeå as "gender-equal"; a second, based on built practices; and a third (including a painting and a "guided bus tour with gender glasses"), which they describe as "*performing* the gender-(un)equal city" (emphasis added). While acknowledging the particular challenge of integrating feminist theory in planning processes, their study considers the need to assess the pitfalls and possibilities of such interventions in terms of politicization—that is, in terms of "articulations of conflict" (Mouffe 2005). In their view, the third, performative approach has the greatest potential for politicizing gender because it creates "tools" for people to see the "inequality that still prevails" (Rönnblom and Sandberg 2015: 15; see also Sandberg and Rönnblom 2014).

Making (up) "developed" and "developing" "places"

The terms "developed" and "developing" describe states of being (see Chapter 6) commonly ascribed to specific countries or regions in national and international policy development. As with the other sections in this chapter, several WPR applications illustrate how approaching "development" as a "complex of practices and knowledges" opens up new ways of thinking about world politics (Walters in Tietäväinen et al. 2008: 64).

For example, Marshall (2012a) highlights how the conditions problematized through notions of "developing" or "undeveloped"—"mostly what was perceived as poverty and backwardness" in Asia, Africa, and Latin America (Escobar 2011: 6)—implicitly privilege Western standards. In addition, Fernandez (2012: 57) argues that a particular problematization of "poverty" as "lack of income" is involved in how "developing places" are constituted (see also Chapter 6 on "poverty"). Her particular example is a major anti-poverty policy in India—the *Swarnajayanti Gram Swarozgar Yojana* (SGSY) —introduced in 1999. Constituting "poverty" as "lack of income", she argues, silences the inequitable distribution of power and access to resources. The accompanying proposal to reduce poverty by organizing the "rural poor", specifically women, into self-help groups, creates "subjects" held to be responsible for their own welfare (Fernandez 2012: 1, 157). Statistics, i.e., the BLP [Below the Poverty Line] census of "poor families" used by the Indian government, *firm up* this "reality", transforming a political issue into a technical one (Fernandez 2012: 58).

Along related lines Calvo (2013) shows how, in European Union policy on "development cooperation" (e.g., AID), the "problem" of "gender equality" is tied closely to pervasive understandings of "poverty reduction" and "economic growth". For countries to become "developed", women have to be assisted to match "men's standard" of labor force participation (Calvo 2013: 154–155). Gender equality, thus, is constituted as a "tool for development", with women produced as either victims or "resources" (see Chapter 4). These kinds of analyses undo the certainty of "developed" and "developing" "places".

Making (up) "public places"

Everyday policy-making necessarily engages with the creation and monitoring of designated places available for public use. A poststructural perspective requires that attention be directed to the ongoing production of these "public spaces" through governmental technologies and rationalities. As with the other "entities" scrutinized in this chapter, the objective is to put in question practices that appear to be reasonable and neutral, highlighting their political character.

For example, Bacchi (2009: 115–117) explores how "public space" is constituted in a series of UK laws, referred to collectively as *Anti-Social Behaviour Orders* (ASBOs), introduced between 1998 and 2003. One of the behaviors considered to be an offence, "loitering", is taken as exemplary. Loitering is generally understood to mean lingering or "hanging around" in a "public place" without apparent purpose. Anti-loitering laws, indicative of the increased surveillance, regulation and control that characterize contemporary modes of rule, are common throughout the United States and Europe (Doherty et al. 2008: 302). "Youth" are frequently targeted.

The underlying presuppositions—the "unexamined ways of thinking" (Foucault 1994a: 456)—that make loitering a "problem" include: assumptions about the value of productive labor, a certain Christian asceticism, and views about "youth" and "idle hands" (supported by psychological theory), among others. "Public space" is thus constituted as a realm of public order and "useful" activity, "belonging to a homogenous social body", while the "abnormal" are "exiled and spatially segregated" (Razack 2002: 11). Silenced is the increased privatizing and policing of public space that makes "loitering" a more likely occurrence (Doherty et al. 2008; Vasagar 2012) and that buttresses other laws limiting the space available for people who may not fit mainstream behavioral norms. For example, "paperless arrest" laws in Australia's Northern Territory, which disproportionately affect Indigenous peoples, allow arrest without warrant for "public order offenses", such as drunkenness, swearing, playing loud music, etc., in "public places" (see Northern Territory of Australia 2014).

The implications for specific groups are significant. Young people in Victoria (Australia) express concern about being moved on when congregating in public areas, especially from sites where they feel safe (VLRC 2010: 65 in Wilson et al. 2010: 45). In Arizona (USA), constant surveillance, heightened through CCTV, and "enforcement rituals", such as immigration raids, neighborhood sweeps, and racial profiling, limit the access of migrants to "public space" (McDowell and Wonders 2009–2010: 57). Increased monitoring of "public places" also poses particular difficulties for homeless people, who rely heavily on such spaces for social, living, and cultural purposes (Middendorp 2002; Doherty et al. 2008). This said, "challenging the rules of legitimacy regarding use of public space" can and does occur (Casey et al. 2007: 93; Zufferey 2014).

Adopting the terms "developed", "developing", "nation-state", "public place", and so on may seem to be a fairly innocuous practice. However, becoming attuned to how these categories have emerged, their grounding assumptions and their effects, brings a cautionary note to their deployment (Bacchi 1996). Indeed, drawing on Mol's (2002) argument that research *makes* realities (see Chapter 2), it can be argued that unquestioning use of these categories supports and entrenches their existence as "real" and immutable, reducing the possibility of contestation (see Bacchi and Rönnblom 2014). As Walters (2009: 487) points out, "debates about the frontiers of Europe are unavoidably political interventions which interject elements of fixture into the fluid and ambiguous space that is Europe". In this circumstance, it seems wise to indicate that the use of these terms, where unavoidable, is provisional. Scare quotes, which at times can appear to be a clumsy intervention, signals this intent. Beyond such a caveat, the WPR approach, as exemplified in this chapter, provides an effective form of analysis to de-naturalize taken-for-granted "places" and other "objects"—to loosen "the grip" of their "present facticity" (Shapiro 1992: 12)—and to highlight the politics involved in their creation.

Notes

1. Applications of WPR in EU Vocational Education Training (Cort 2008) and in the Erasmus Mundus Master's Program (Papatsiba 2014) confirm the operation of an underlying economic rationality in European policy processes.
2. See Doel (2000) on approaching "space" (and we would add "place") as a verb instead of as a noun, treating it as an action or event. See also McDowell and Wonders (2009–2010) on "mobile border performances".

CHAPTER 8

Conclusion

Abstract The Conclusion provides an overview of the main points developed in the book. It includes a brief synopsis of each chapter and highlights the usefulness of the WPR approach for those involved in policy development. The key premises of the approach are summarized to facilitate application.

Keywords "problems" · discourse · governmentality · neoliberalism · strategies · resistance

This book introduces a Foucault-influenced approach to poststructural policy analysis and explains the usefulness of this perspective for those wishing to engage in critical policy analysis. It offers a user-friendly "tool" to conduct poststructural policy analysis, called "What's the Problem Represented to be?" (WPR approach). Applications of the approach by policy workers/analysts illustrate its potential for disrupting conventional views about the meaning of policy and how governing takes place.

The WPR approach brings together several Foucauldian modes of inquiry, including archaeology, genealogy, and problematization, to generate a range of new questions for policy workers/analysts. These new questions provide guidelines for thinking about policy development at a level uncommonly probed—the deep-seated presuppositions and assumptions that underpin policies and the ways in which policies

C. Bacchi, S. Goodwin, *Poststructural Policy Analysis*,
DOI 10.1057/978-1-137-52546-8_8

actively produce, or constitute, "problems", "subjects", "objects", and "places" in specific contexts. This innovative approach to policy analysis puts in question the taken-for-granted view prevalent among many who develop, implement, and analyze policies that policy problems are self-evident, and that subjects, objects, and places simply exist. It facilitates critical policy analysis through creating the possibility of thinking otherwise.

The book has two parts. Part I locates the particular poststructural approach introduced in the book within other recent developments in the policy analysis field and elaborates its theoretical grounding. Chapter 1 sets the scene. It provides a brief synopsis of the Foucauldian version of poststructuralism that guides the analysis in subsequent chapters. It also highlights the importance of this stance for how policy work is thought about and practiced, emphasizing the possibility of critical engagement and contestation.

Chapter 2 introduces the WPR approach and explains the forms of criticism it involves. The approach, as elaborated there, encourages critical interrogation of policy proposals through six questions and an undertaking to apply those questions to one's own proposals (see WPR Chart on page 20). Importantly, a WPR analysis does not offer firm solutions to assumed problems. Rather, it encourages policy workers to reflect on how policy "problems" are produced (or represented) within the policies and policy proposals they develop and implement.

The argument, introduced in Chapter 2 and developed throughout the book, is that governing takes place *through* the ways in which "problems" are represented in policies (problem representations). This view of how governing occurs brings a new urgency to consideration of how "problems" are constituted within policies, the unexamined forms of thinking they rely upon, the practices that generate them and the effects they produce. The term "effects" captures the ways in which particular problem representations limit what can be thought (discursive effects), affect what it is possible for people to become (subjectification effects) and impact on how they live their lives (lived effects). Probing problem representations for these effects becomes a politically efficacious task, opening up consideration of alternative problematizations of a wide range of social issues.

Chapter 3 introduces key theoretical concepts in Foucault-influenced poststructural analysis. The chapter contains seven subsections, each of which is dedicated to a group of related concepts. These subsections assist readers to grasp what it means to:

- talk about power as productive;
- take practices as a starting point for analysis;
- focus on discourses as knowledges;
- examine governmental problematizations;
- adopt a governmentality perspective;
- carry out Foucauldian-style genealogies;
- put in question the humanist subject.

The chapter, thus, provides a resource for policy analysts interested in using the WPR approach by outlining direct links between Foucauldian themes and concepts, and the WPR questions.

Part II of the book illustrates the forms of critical analysis made possible through Foucault-influenced poststructuralism, and specifically, through application of the WPR approach. It draws on the work of a diverse array of policy workers/analysts from many countries who have used the questions in the approach to examine critically a wide range of policy developments. These examples of application have been organized around four themes—making and unmaking "problems", "subjects", "objects", and "places".

The uniting argument that these "things" have been made—and hence can be unmade—finds its inspiration in the poststructural thinking that underpins the book. In a poststructural perspective things that are commonly taken for granted as real and unchanging (e.g., nations, public places, addiction), including the presumed fixed nature of human subjects and groups of human subjects (e.g., youth, irregular migrants), are seen as generated in repeated heterogeneous practices and relations. They are *made*. Activity is involved in their becoming. Hence, they are political creations rather than inescapable ways of being or facts of life.

The analytic task, therefore, becomes drawing attention to the politics involved in their emergence as "the real"—how it was possible for these things to come to be—making that politics visible. Politics here is understood to comprise the plural practices involved in the coming to be of "things". By denaturalizing "things" in this way, they are opened up for possible modification—they can be *unmade*—should they be found to produce detrimental consequences for specific groups of people or for life in general.

Chapter 4 elaborates what it means to say that "problems" are constituted in policies. It traces and contests how "problems" are conceptualized in a range of policy theories, including classic rationalist, interpretive and critical realist approaches. From this starting place it demonstrates how select applications of the WPR approach put into question "problems" presumed to exist in drug and alcohol policy, and gender equality policy.

Chapter 5 confronts the challenging task of rethinking how "subjects" are conceptualized in the policies that purportedly address them. The view that subjects exist as particular kinds of people (rational, self-sufficient, risk averse, caring, lazy) independently of policy is countered with illustrations of how "subjects" are constituted *within* policies that allocate specific subject positions for them to occupy. "Subjects" become provisional, in ongoing formation, emphasizing the importance of examining policies for how they produce "subjects". WPR applications that undertake this task are drawn from the following fields: education policy, health policy, immigration policy, economic policy, transport policy, environment policy, and disability/equality policy.

Chapter 6 calls upon readers to rethink the nature of "objects". Instead of presumed, fixed "entities", they emerge as "objectivizations" produced in policy. The point of this form of intervention is to encourage policy workers/analysts to interrogate presumed "objects that exist" and show how, through problematization, they are given specific characteristics and associations. The postulated "singularity of objects" turns out to be "an accomplishment," an act of "coordination" (Mol 2002: 7–8), with research methods identified as major players in the reinforcement of particular realities. On these grounds, the applications of WPR in this chapter call for a rethinking of the commonly assumed policy objects of "poverty", "addiction", "literacy", and "wellbeing".

Chapter 7 elaborates the implications of taking assumed geographical entities—"places"—for granted as specific kinds of "objects". Further, it illustrates, through selected WPR applications, how poststructural policy analysis draws attention to the multitude of practices that need to be repeated on a daily basis for certain "sites" to emerge as "real". In the process this form of analysis produces opportunities to challenge the assumed facticity of "states", "regions", "public places", etc.

The Appendix, by Bacchi and Bonham, offers a poststructural methodology for analyzing interviews. Policy analysts commonly draw on interview material to provide background or on-the-ground perspectives on specific developments. Since poststructuralism puts in question "subjects" as sources of "true" information based on "direct" experience, it is necessary to approach interviews differently from forms of analysis that rest on these premises. PIA [Poststructural Interview Analysis] offers a way to locate interview comments within the practices that generate them and thus to politicize what tends to be treated as "truth", including assumptions about interviewees themselves as sources of truth. To this end, it draws upon key theoretical concepts introduced in the book, including genealogy and discursive practices. The research task becomes interrogating how specific "things said" come to be said, and how transformation is possible.

Throughout the book, the WPR approach is proposed as an accessible and adaptable guide to poststructural policy analysis through seven interrelated forms of questioning and analysis. The six questions enable analysts to select a specific policy or governmental technology, and to interrogate it in ways that reveal levels of complexity that require consideration. They provoke specific forms of political engagement, encouraging analysts to reflect on possible alternative problematizations. At the same time a practice of self-problematization, endorsed in the undertaking to apply the WPR questions to one's own proposals or recommendations, alerts researchers to their participation in ontological politics, *making* rather than *reflecting* "reality" (Chapter 2). The ethos of continual criticism thus promoted opens up the space for challenge and protest.

The WPR approach, however, needs to be used carefully. Some key premises that can sometimes slip away in the process of analysis are summarized here:

- Usually the terms "problem" and "problems" are placed in scare quotes to signal that their commonly assumed status as fixed and readily identifiable "entities" is put in question. Departure from this practice occurs only where it is clear that a particular theoretical stance, such as positivism, treats problems as straightforward and uncontentious (see Chapter 1, endnote 1, p. 12).
- Analysis begins from proposals or proposed solutions and researchers "read off" the implicit problem representations within them.
- References to governing include but extend beyond the state to encompass a wide range of agencies and people involved in societal administration.
- The term "discourse" refers to background knowledge, and "discourses" are knowledges rather than forms of language use.
- "Subjects" are provisional and in ongoing formation, rather than stable kinds of being.

- Governmentalities, such as neoliberalism, are not monolithic and determining rationalities, nor ideologies.
- Resistance does not sit outside power, meaning that forms of protest might also involve forms of complicity.
- References to strategies and "strategic relations" describe complex societal relations and practices rather than intentional manipulation.
- Poststructural policy analysis aims to study, not people's views, but how it is possible for such views to exist.

In terms of political vision, the perspective developed in this book is valuable for what it opens up rather than for what it proscribes (Moss 1998: 9). It does not put forward a blueprint for political change, which people are expected to adopt, but instead aims to "craft a different kind of political space in which critics can operate" (Brown 1998: 34). In tune with Foucault's own "version of emancipation", universals are replaced with "specific transformations" that minimize domination (Moss 1998: 9). In line with this view the WPR approach consists of *questions*, not directives. As the sub-title for the book suggests, it is a *guide* to practice. With the WPR approach as guide, policy workers/analysts become "policy problematizers" (Webb 2014: 371). They are spurred to reflect on the presuppositions underpinning specific policy proposals, including their own proposals. They are prompted, further, to reflect on alternative ways of constituting "problems", and on how alternative problematizations may produce new "subjects", different "objects", and other ways of imagining political space.

As illustrated in the applications in the book, the WPR approach has proved popular with policy workers/analysts. Clearly, there is a significant section of the policy community eager to embrace the form of critical analysis it offers. The applications also indicate the popularity of the approach among research students, who are often also policy workers, in a wide range of policy fields. These and other scholars find the WPR questions helpful in generating and structuring useful research projects (Manning 2014; Bletsas and Beasley 2012). By making the approach more accessible, this book produces poststructural policy analysis in a form that people can employ and enjoy.

Appendix

Poststructural Interview Analysis: Politicizing "personhood"

*Carol Bacchi and Jennifer Bonham**

Abstract This Appendix introduces a new poststructural approach to interview analysis. It outlines seven closely related processes that address the following questions:

- precisely what is said in the interview?
- how was it or is it possible to say those things?
- which networks of relations (discursive practices) are relevant to the interview topic?
- what do the selected "things said" produce as "subjects", "objects", and "places"?
- how do the interviewers and interviewees problematize "what they are, what they do, and the world in which they live" (Foucault, 1986)?
- which "things said" put in question pervasive ways of thinking?
- what political consequences follow from interviewers' selection and distribution practices?

Keywords "things said" · politicization · "regimes of truth" · discursive practices · subject positions · transformation · distribution

---

*Jennifer Bonham is Senior Lecturer, Department of Geography, Environment and Population, The University of Adelaide.

C. Bacchi, S. Goodwin, *Poststructural Policy Analysis*,
DOI 10.1057/978-1-137-52546-8

Interviewing is one of the most common social science methodologies. Many books and articles (Holstein and Gubrium 2003; Alvesson 2011) describe a range of interview techniques – "expert", "semi-structured", "in-depth", etc. Cautions are raised about power relations in interview settings, specifically between interviewers and interviewees, with accompanying ethical concerns (Fontana and Frey 2005). Less attention is directed to the "subject" who is assumed as a starting place when drawing on interview material (but see Hanna et al. 2015).

In a general sense it seems fair to say that interview subjects are considered to have privileged ("first person") access to a kind of "truth" about their "experience/s". This view of a "founding subject"—a person who pre-exists society and who "grasps intuitively" the meanings within "empty things" (Foucault 1972: 227)—poses difficulties for poststructural researchers who wish to use interviews as part of their analysis. St. Pierre (2011: 620) describes the quandary thus: "[I]f we no longer believe in a disentangled humanist self, individual, person, we have to rethink qualitative methods (interviewing and observation) grounded in that human being as well as humanist representation".

While some poststructuralists remain skeptical of the redeeming possibilities of research interviews (Fadyl and Nicholls 2013), others have used them to challenge discourses both in relation to the "self" and at the broader societal level (see for example Gibson et al. 2008). Others (e.g., Laurier and Philo 2004; Stern 2006; Moisander et al. 2009; Davis 2010; Holstein and Gubrium 2011) have combined poststructuralist insights with ethnomethodology to examine how individuals make sense of their lives. However, as Jones (1997) and Bastalich (2009) demonstrate, much of the research in this vein reintroduces the founding subject of humanism.

To move past this obstacle to poststructural use of interview material, a methodology, referred to as Poststructural Interview Analysis (PIA), is outlined below (see also Bonham et al. 2015). This methodology is solidly grounded in Foucauldian-influenced thinking and draws on the theory and concepts introduced in Chapter 3. An initial premise is that interviews, like all knowledge practices, including conventional policy studies, are inherently political. The analytic task, therefore, becomes providing support to practitioners in developing alternative approaches to a program or project they wish to challenge.

Practices in Foucault (1991b: 75) are "places" where "what is said and what is done ... meet and interconnect". A practice is the routine enactment of relations between things—e.g., all of the elements which make up a clinical diagnosis from the hospital gurney and stethoscope to the question "does it hurt when ... ?". In the place of "founding subjects" assumed to have a deep "inner" core of being, practices produce "subjects" as subjects of particular kinds. Moreover, since practices are multiple and ongoing, "subjects" are always in process—fluid and relational—rather than fixed essences of any sort. Hence, "subjects" are provisional and opportunities for modification are many.[1]

This particular approach to "subjects" as "in process" makes it possible to treat interviews—or more precisely interview transcripts—as texts. The procedure to deal with these texts involves a form of "de-*person*-alization", or—to put it more positively—a form of *politicization* of "personhood". To reiterate, we are not concerned with understanding why the interviewee says what s/he says or analyzing the kind of "subject" an interviewee has become. Rather we are interested in mapping the kinds of "subject" it is possible to become. A major purpose of the analysis is to consider the particular kinds of "subjects" produced within interview settings, while also reflecting on how subject status can be questioned and disrupted. This brief introduction to PIA is intended to indicate how such analysis can be performed, and why it is useful. To make the approach more accessible, seven "processes" are introduced, though the interconnected nature of the analysis needs to be highlighted.

Process 1: Noting "*what* is said"

PIA bypasses concerns about people's (assumed) motives or intentions in interviews. Instead, the analysis begins by examining *precisely* "*what* is said"—the "things said". To avoid confusion with language studies, it is important to emphasize that the interest here is not in "what *people* say", but in "*what* people say", in "*exactly* what is said" (Veyne 1997: 156; emphasis in original).

Much of what is said in an interview appears as nothing new, as common knowledge (*savoir*) or common sense. It is important to notice and note such "things said" as they often have normative implications, establishing ways for people to be. Particular attention should be paid to moments of "excision and attribution", "measurement", and "self-formation". Excision and attribution refer to "points in the interview where particular ways of thinking, feeling, characterising and doing are differentiated from the mass of existence", measurement to "those moments where some form of quantification is used", and self-formation to those moments when the interviewee speaks of the self in terms of an available subject position, consequently "binding the self to that position" (see Bonham et al. 2015: 189).

"Things said" have greater or lesser import and impact depending upon the institutional location of those who say them and in what context—i.e., depending on the status or authority accorded certain "things said" (see also Process 3). For example, discourses (knowledges) with strong institutional mechanisms, such as medical discourses, are likely to carry more force than those with fewer such mechanisms, such as the home birth movement (Bacchi and Eveline 2010: 158).

Research questions include:

- What "things said" have been noted?
- On what grounds have they been noted?

Process 2: Producing Genealogies of "*What* is said"

Reflecting on selected "things said" it becomes important to consider how it was or is possible to say those things, how they are rendered "say*able*" (Foucault 1991a: 59). That is, analysts need to reflect on how "*what* is said" *could be* said—how they are considered to be legitimate or "truthful" things to say. To this end it is necessary to produce histories (Foucault 1991a: 64), or more precisely genealogies, of "things said".

Such genealogies look to identify the "conditions" necessary in a particular period "for this or that enunciation to be formulated" (Foucault 1972: 15 fn 2). Attention is directed to the multitudes of practices—the "processes, procedures and apparatuses" (Tamboukou 1999: 202)—involved in the production of "*what* is said" as "sayable", as "within the true". Take, for example, the comments "I felt depressed" or "We work with mental trauma". The political target is not how psychology or psychiatry control or label people but all the interconnected practices that make depression and mental trauma apparent and intelligible, and give these knowledge formations authority.

In PIA, therefore, "things said" are analyzed in terms of the practices that give rise to them. For example, attention shifts from the assumed attributes of individuals to the genealogy of those "attributes". Asking "What is it possible to speak of?" (Foucault 1991a: 59) provides a novel and powerful form of political analysis, showing how political practice takes part in the "conditions of emergence, insertion and functioning" of "regimes of truth" (Foucault 1972: 163).

Some research questions include:

- What meanings need to be in place for particular "things said" to be intelligible?
- Where and how has a specific "thing said" come to be accepted as "truth"?

Process 3: Highlighting Key Discursive Practices

Foucault referred to the sets, or networks, of heterogeneous relations that install "regimes of truth" as *discursive practices* or *dispositifs* (Bacchi and Bonham 2014). Discourse in Foucault refers to knowledge, and discourses are described as practices (Foucault 1991a). *Discursive practice* encapsulates *how* discourses "practice", how they operate to establish their knowledge credentials. For example, Foucault (1972: 41) elucidates how "psychiatric discourse finds a way of limiting its domain, of defining what it is talking about, giving it [its domain] the status of an object—and therefore of making it manifest, nameable, and describable".

Discursive practices are not concerned with language or logical propositions. Rather, they involve relations among heterogeneous elements including, but not limited to, actions, symbols, materials, words, and gestures. It is possible to "map" notionally the "elements"—e.g., the sites, subject positions (kinds of subjects and authority of those subjects), practices, objects, actions, and interactions in a discursive practice (see Bacchi and Bonham 2014: 186; "Field of Dispersion of Population Statements"). It is through the ongoing enactment of relations within discursive practices that "subjects", "objects", and "places" are in continual formation.

Interviews operate in and through a plethora of discursive practices—e.g., the discursive practices of health, transport, biology, migration, and so on. Hence, it is necessary to consider how the specific discursive practices relevant to the interview topic generate things that can be said "within the true". Analysts pay particular attention to the normative implications of identified discursive practices. As examples, consider the effects of privileging "mobility" within a transport discursive practice, or "fitness" within a health discursive practice. Analysts look also to identify the subject positions—the characteristics, behaviors, and dispositions which constitute particular kinds of subjects—within those practices, e.g., the mobile subject, the healthy citizen, etc. It is also important to pay attention to the interview process as a site within a discursive practice, participating in setting norms for behavior and making available the subject positions of "interviewer" and "interviewee".

Research questions include:

- Which discursive practices are relevant to the "things said" that are the focus of the analysis?
- Which subject positions are made available within these discursive practices?

Process 4: Analyzing "*what* is said"

"Things said" have important functions in installing certain norms and subject positions. They play a critical role in forming "subjects", "objects", and "places", and giving authority to certain discursive practices. Hence, they need to be studied in terms of what they *produce*, or constitute, rather than in terms of what they "mean".

For example, a comment such as "women are less inclined to take risks" produces "women" as risk averse. Or, a comment that "I don't have the skill for that job" produces "skills" as human attributes, and as *required* human attributes (required for the job). Similarly, a reference such as "I always celebrate Australia Day" produces "Australia" as a legitimate spatial entity given the endorsement of a national public holiday.

Research questions include:

- Which norms do the "things said" invoke?
- Which "subjects" are produced?
- Which "objects" do they create?
- Which "places" are produced as legitimate?

Process 5: Interrogating the Production of "subjects"

Interviews are important resources for considering how we are continually produced as particular kinds of provisional subjects. Foucault (1986: 10) offered problematization as a theoretical intervention in exploring the production of "subjects"—studying "the conditions in which human beings 'problematize' what they are, what they do, and the world in which they live". Research interviews provide access to such problematization practices.

Interviewers, for instance, call upon interviewees to examine their being, to differentiate and scrutinize elements of their lives, then to position these elements in relation to each other and in relation to the lives of others. In the process, interviewees *problematize* their conduct in terms of established norms and in doing so associate themselves with certain subject positions. By analyzing exactly what interviewees say ("*what* is said"), therefore, it becomes possible to reflect on the criteria and processes by which they differentiate themselves as particular kinds of subjects, how they come to occupy specific subject positions and how they open spaces to disrupt those positions. In this way PIA shifts the focus from the founding or fixed subject to the processes through which "individuals" become entangled in discursive practices, and the mechanisms by which "individuals" acknowledge themselves as particular types of subjects.[2]

Research questions include:

- "What" does the individual relate to the self?
- What ways of moving, thinking, characterizing and feeling has the interviewee excised and related to the self?
- In which discursive practices have these attributes been, and continue to be, formed?

Process 6: Exploring Transformative Potential

Recalling that, in poststructuralism, the kind of subject that one can become is "in process" (see above), then by focusing exactly on "*what* is said" it becomes possible to use interview material to explore mutations in subject positions. Discursive practices are plural and, at times, contradictory, opening up spaces for disruption. Interview material can, therefore, serve as a political resource to analyze transformative potential.

The following research questions highlight how certain comments ("*what* is said") can provide the basis for contesting prevailing discourses:

- Does a particular interviewee comment appear unusual, inappropriate or out of context?
- Does a particular comment offer an alternative to a taken-for-granted "reality"?

Process 7: Questioning the Politics of Distribution

Interviewers play a critical role in the political uses of interview material. Beyond the ethical complications of different types and levels of authority afforded to the interviewer and interviewee, interviewers exercise power as they distinguish what will be reported, what will be included/excluded, and how and where it will be distributed. Quantitative-based interviews (such as surveys) also operate to limit "*what* is said" as they often restrict responses to what a given discipline already deems to be appropriate. The political import of research "findings" derives from the truth status attached to such findings and the breadth of dispersion of such findings, including research publications, conferences, discipline seminars, workshops, media reporting, and policy discussions.

The following questions address the role of the researcher in producing, analyzing and distributing "*what* is said":

- Do particular interviewer comments ("things said") challenge or reinforce pervasive ways of thinking?
- Do the questions asked (either in a survey or in a semi-structured interview) function to reinforce or challenge pervasive ways of thinking?
- Are the sites for distributing research results constrained in ways that reinforce pervasive ways of thinking?

Concluding Comment

To some analysts PIA may appear to undermine the individual integrity of interviewees. Indeed, they may find its "de*person*alizing" strategy offensive. However, the purpose of the approach is to highlight the contingency and politics involved in shaping the kind of person it is possible to become—to *politicize* "personhood" —and hence to increase opportunities for contestation.

In the place of the view that the world consists (simply) of a particular type of person (one *with* emotions, affects, etc.) or types of people (women, men, youth, migrants, who behave in predictable ways) it directs attention to the heterogeneous strategic relations and practices involved in making what appear to be self-evident traits and dispositions possible. This foregrounding of the practices that produce "*what* is said" as "truth" brings a heightened political sensitivity to interview analysis. It signals that "reality" is *made* in and through discursive practices and that, given the plurality and mutability of those practices, it can be *unmade*.

Notes

1. The use of quotation marks, called scare quotes, around "subject" and "subjects", signals their provisional status; "subjects" are always "works in progress".
2. "Individuals" are provisional in the same ways as "subjects". The term "acknowledge" does not refer to a purposive volitional state of mind but simply to the activity of taking up a particular subject position – e.g., ticking the box "male" or "female" on a form.

Bibliography

Aitken, R. (2006). Performativity, popular finance and security in the global political economy. In M. de Goede (Ed.), *International political economy and poststructural politics*. Basingstoke: Palgrave Macmillan.

Alexander, S., & Coveney, J. (2013). A critical discourse analysis of Canadian and Australian public health recommendations promoting physical activity to children. *Health Sociology Review*, *22* (4), 353–364.

Allan, E. (2012). *Policy discourses, gender, and education: Constructing women's status*. New York: Routledge.

Alvesson, M. (2011). *Interpreting interviews*. London: Sage.

Alvesson, M., & Sandberg, J. (2013). *Constructing research questions: Doing interesting research*. London: Sage.

American Psychiatric Association (2013). *Substance-related and addictive disorders*. Arlington, VA: American Psychiatric Publishing.

ANCD (2012). *1st Recovery Roundtable Report*. Canberra: Australian National Council on Drugs.

Anderson, S., & Berglund, K. (2012). Part I: Policies for innovation. In S. Anderson, K. Berglund, E. Gunnarsson, E. Sundin (Eds.), *Promoting innovation: Policies, practises and procedures*, VINNOVA Report VR 2012.08, Swedish Governmental Agency for Innovation System, Stockholm.

Anderson, S., Berglund, K., Gunnarsson, E., Sundin, E. (eds) (2012). *Promoting innovation: Policies, practices and procedures*, VINNOVA Report VR 2012.08, Swedish Governmental Agency for Innovation System, Stockholm, http://www.vinnova.se/upload/EPiStorePDF/vr_12_08.pdf, Accessed 20 November 2015.

Armstrong, E. (2007). Moral panic over meth. *Contemporary Justice Review*, *10* (4), 427–442.

C. Bacchi, S. Goodwin, *Poststructural Policy Analysis*,
DOI 10.1057/978-1-137-52546-8

Ashley, R.K. (1988). Untying the sovereign state: A double reading of the anarchy problematique. *Millennium: Journal of International Studies, 17* (2), 227–262.

Australian Commonwealth Government (2005). *Government response to: Senate Community Affairs References Committee Report on poverty and financial hardship "A hand up not a hand out": Renewing the fight against poverty.* Canberra: Australian Government.

Australian Government (2007). *Changing behaviour: A public policy perspective.* Canberra: Australian Public Service Commission.

Australian Public Service Commission (2007). *Tackling wicked problems: A public policy perspective.* Canberra: Australian Government.

Bacchi, C. (1996). *The politics of affirmative action: "Women", equality and category politics.* London: Sage.

Bacchi, C. (1999). *Women, policy and politics: The construction of policy problems.* London: Sage.

Bacchi, C. (2009). *Analysing policy: What's the problem represented to be?* Frenchs Forest: Pearson Education.

Bacchi, C. (2011). Gender mainstreaming and reflexivity: Asking some hard questions, Keynote address, Advancing Gender + Training in Theory and Practice, Conference at Complutense University, Madrid, 3 February 2011.

Bacchi, C. (2012). Why study problematizations? Making politics visible. *Open Journal of Political Science, 2* (1), 1–8.

Bacchi, C. (2015a). The turn to problematization: Political implications of contrasting interpretive and poststructural adaptations. *Open Journal of Political Science, 5*, 1–12.

Bacchi, C. (2015b). Problematizations in alcohol policy: WHO's "alcohol problems". *Contemporary Drug Problems, 42* (2), 130–147.

Bacchi, C. (2016a). Policies as gendering practices: Re-viewing categorical distinctions, *Journal of Women, Politics and Policy*, DOI:10.1080/1554477X.2016.1198207.

Bacchi, C. (2016b). Problematizations in health policy: Questioning how "problems" are constituted in policies. SAGE *Open*, DOI:10.1177/2158244016653986.

Bacchi, C., & Bonham, J. (2014). Reclaiming discursive practices as an analytic focus: Political implications. *Foucault Studies, 17*, 173–192.

Bacchi, C., & Eveline, J. (eds) (2010). *Mainstreaming politics: Gendering practices and feminist theory.* Adelaide: University of Adelaide Press.

Bacchi, C., & Rönnblom, M. (2014). Feminist discursive institutionalism—A poststructural alternative. *NORA – Nordic Journal of Feminist and Gender Research*, DOI: 10.1080/08038740.2013.864701.

Ball, S.J. (1990). *Politics and policy making in education: Explorations in policy sociology.* New York: Routledge.

Ball, S.J. (1993). What is policy? Texts, trajectories and toolboxes. *Discourse: Studies in the Cultural Politics of Education*, *13* (2), 10–17.

Ball, S.J. (1997). Policy sociology and critical social research: A personal review of recent education policy and policy research. *British Educational Research Journal*, *23* (3), 257–274.

Ball, S.J. (2015). What is policy? 21 years later: Reflections on the possibilities of policy research. *Discourse: Studies in the Cultural Politics of Education*, *36* (3), 306–313.

Bambra, C., Smith, K. E., Garthwaite, K., Joyce, K.D., Hunter, D.J. (2011). A labour of Sisyphus? Public policy and health inequalities research from the Black and Acheson Reports to the Marmot Review. *Journal of Epidemiology & Community Health*, *65* (5), 399–406.

Bastalich, W. (2009). Reading Foucault: Genealogy and social science research and methodology. *Social Research Online*, *14* (2).

Bastian, A., & Coveney, J. (2013). The responsibilisation of food security: What is the problem represented to be? *Health Sociology Review*, *22* (2), 162–173.

Bernauer, J.W. (1992). *Michel Foucault's force of flight: Toward an ethics for thought*. New Jersey: Humanities Press.

Bhabha, H. (1984). Of mimicry and man: The ambivalence of colonial discourse. *October* (Spring), *28*, 125–133.

Bigo, D. (2002). Security and immigration: Toward a critique of the governmentality of unease. *Alternatives: Global, Local, Political*, *27*, 63–92.

Bjørnholt, M. (2012). From work-sharing couples to equal parents: Changing perspectives of men and gender equality. In C. Krekula, M. Åberg, M.J. Samuelsson (Eds.), *Gender and change: Power, politics and everyday practices*. Karlstad: Karlstad University Press.

Bletsas, A. (2007). Contesting representations of poverty: Ethics and evaluation. *Policy & Society*, *26* (3), 65–83.

Bletsas, A. (2012). Spaces between: Elaborating the theoretical underpinnings of the "WPR" approach and its significance for contemporary scholarship. In A. Bletsas, & C. Beasley (Eds.), *Engaging with Carol Bacchi: Strategic interventions and exchanges*. Adelaide: University of Adelaide Press.

Bletsas, A., & Beasley, C. (2012). *Engaging with Carol Bacchi: Strategic interventions and exchanges*. Adelaide: University of Adelaide Press.

Bletsas, A., & Michell, D. (2014). Classism on campus: Explaining and extending understandings of social class in the contemporary higher education debates. In H. Brook, D. Fergie, M. Maeorg, D. Michell (Eds.), *Universities in transition: Foregrounding social contexts of knowledge in the first year experience*. Adelaide: University of Adelaide Press.

Bonham, J. (2006). Transport: Disciplining the body that travels. *The Sociological Review*, *54* (Issue Supplement s1), 57–74.

Bonham, J., Bacchi, C., Wanner, T. (2015). Gender and cycling: Gendering cycling subjects and *forming* bikes, practices and spaces as gendered objects. In J. Bonham, & M. Johnson (Eds.), *Cycling futures*. Adelaide: University of Adelaide Press.

Bordo, S. (2003). *Unbearable weight: Feminism, western culture, and the body*. California: University of California Press.

Bottrell, D., & Goodwin, S. (2011). Contextualising schools and communities. In D. Bottrell, & S. Goodwin (Eds.), *Schools, communities and social inclusion*. South Yarra: Palgrave Macmillan.

Bradley, D., Noonan, P., Nugent, H., Scales, B. (2008). *Review of Australian Higher Education, Final Report*. Canberra: Department of Education, Employment and Workplace Relations.

Brown, W. (1998). Genealogical politics. In J. Moss (Ed.), *The later Foucault: Politics and philosophy*. London: Sage.

Burkett, I., & Sheehan, G. (2009). *From the margins to the mainstream: The challenges for microfinance in Australia*. Melbourne: Brotherhood of St. Lawrence/Foresters Community Finance.

Butler, J. (1993). *Bodies that matter: On the discursive limits of "sex"*. New York: Routledge.

Callon, M., & Latour, B. (1981). Unscrewing the big Leviathan: How actors macro-structure reality and how sociologists help them to do so. In K.D. Knorr-Cetina, & A. Cicourel (Eds.), *Advances in social theory and methodology: Towards an integration of micro and macro-sociology*. London: Routledge and Kegan Paul.

Calvo, D. (2013). *What is the problem of gender? Mainstreaming gender in migration and development in the European Union*, PhD Thesis, Department of Sociology and Work Science, University of Gothenburg.

Carrington, K., & Watson, P. (1996). Policing sexual violence: Feminism, criminal justice and governmentality. *International Journal of the Sociology of Law*, *24* (3), 253–272.

Carson, L., & Edwards, K. (2011). Prostitution and sex trafficking: What are the problems represented to be? A discursive analysis of law and policy in Sweden and Victoria, Australia. *The Australian Feminist Law Journal*, *34*, 63–87.

Carter, P.M. (2013). Poststructuralist theory and sociolinguistics: Mapping the linguistic turn in social theory. *Language and Linguistics Compass*, *7* (11), 580–596.

Casey, R., Goudie, R., Reeve, K. (2007). Resistance and identity: Homeless women's use of public spaces. *People, Place & Policy Online*, *1* (2), 90–97. DOI: 10.3351/ppp.0001.0002.0005.

Chia, R. (1996). The problem of reflexivity in organizational research: Towards a postmodern science of organization. *Organization*, *3* (1), 31–59.

Clarke, J., & Newman, J. (2009). Elusive publics: Knowledge, power and public service reform. In S. Gewirtz, P. Mahony, I. Hextall, A. Cribb (Eds.),

Changing teacher professionalism: International trends, challenges, and ways forward. UK: Routledge.

Clifford, M. (2001). *Political genealogy after Foucault: Savage identities*. New York: Routledge.

Clough, P.T. (2007). Notes towards a theory of affect-itself. *Ephemera: Theory & Politics in Organization*, *7*, 60–77.

Coffey, A. (2004). *Reconceptualizing social policy: Sociological perspectives on contemporary social policy*. Berkshire: Open University Press.

Cohen, C. (2014). *Male rape is a feminist issue: Feminism, governmentality and male rape*. Basingstoke: Palgrave Macmillan.

Cohen, S. (2002) [1972]. *Folk devils and moral panics: The creation of the mods and rockers*. London and New York: Routledge.

Colebatch, H., Hoppe, R., Noordegraaf, M. (2010). The lessons for policy work. In H. Colebatch, R. Hoppe, M. Noordgraaf (Eds.), *Working for policy*. Amsterdam: Amsterdam University Press.

Cort, P. (2008). VET policy formation and discourse in the EU: A mobile work force for a European labour market. In C.H. Jørgensen, & V. Aarkrog (Eds.), *Divergence and convergence in education and work: Studies in vocational and continuing education*. Bern: Peter Lang.

Council of the European Union (1999). *Schengen acquis*, 1999/435/EC and 1999/436/EC.

Council of the European Union (2004). *EU Drug Strategy 2005–2012*. Brussels.

Davidson, A. (1990). Closing up the corpses. In G. Boulos (Ed.), *Meaning and method*. Cambridge: Cambridge University Press.

Davis, K. (2010). Accounting for disappointment: Biographical choices re-visited, Paper presented at the XVII ISA World Congress of Sociology: The Role of Transnational Public Intellectuals, Gothenburg, Sweden, July, *Biography and Society Newsletter*, 13–16.

Dean, M. (1999). *Governmentality: Power and rule in modern society*. London: Sage.

Dean, M. (2002). A genealogy of the government of poverty. *Economy and Society*, *21* (3), 215–251.

Dean, M., & Hindess, B. (1998). *Governing Australia: Studies in contemporary rationalities of government*. Cambridge: Cambridge University Press.

Death, C. (2006). Resisting (nuclear) power? Environmental regulation in South Africa. *Review of African Political Economy*, *33* (109), 407–424.

Death, C. (2010). Counter-conducts: A Foucauldian analytics of protest. *Social Movement Studies*, *9* (3), 235–251.

de Goede, M. (2006). International political economy and the promises of post-structuralism. In M. de Goede (Ed.), *International political economy and poststructural politics*. Houndmills: Palgrave Macmillan.

Deleuze, G. (1992). *Foucault*. Minneapolis: University of Minnesota Press.

Dery, D. (1984). *Problem definition in policy analysis.* Lawrence, KS: University Press of Kansas.

Dhamoon, R.K. (2011). Considerations on mainstreaming intersectionality. *Political Research Quarterly, 64* (1), 230–243.

Doel, M. (2000). Un-glunking geography: Spatial science after Dr Seuss and Gilles Deleuze. In M. Crang, & N. Thrift (Eds.), *Thinking space.* London and New York: Routledge.

Doherty, J., Busch-Geertsema, V., Karpuskiene, V., Korhonen, J., O'Sullivan, E., Sahlin, I., Tosse, A., Petrillo, A., Wygna, J. (2008). Homelessness and exclusion: Regulating public space in European cities. *Surveillance & Society, 5* (3), 290–314.

Dreyfus, H.L., & Rabinow, P. (1983). *Michel Foucault: Beyond structuralism and hermeneutics*, 2nd edition. Chicago: University of Chicago Press.

du Rose, N. (2015). *The governance of female drug users: Women's experiences of drug policy.* Bristol: Policy Press.

Edwards, K. (2010). Social inclusion: Is this a way forward for young people, and should we go there? *Youth Studies Australia, 29* (2), 16–24.

Elsey, H., Tolhurst, R., Theobald, S. (2005). Mainstreaming HIV/AIDS in development sectors: Have we learnt the lessons from gender mainstreaming? *AIDS Care, 17* (8), 988–998.

Eribon, D. (1991). *Michel Foucault.* London: Faber and Faber.

Escobar, A. (2011). *Encountering development: The making and unmaking of the third world.* Princeton: Princeton University Press.

Eveline, J. (2005). Woman in the Ivory Tower: Gendering feminised and masculinised identities. *Journal of Organizational Change Management, 18* (6), 641–658.

Ewald, F. (1991). Insurance and risk. In G. Burchell, C. Gordon, P. Miller (Eds.), *The Foucault effect: Studies in governmentality.* Hemel Hempstead: Harvester Wheatsheaf.

Ezzamel, M., & Willmott, H. (2009). Strategy and strategizing: A poststructuralist perspective. *The Globalization of Strategy Research, Advances in Strategic Management, 27*, 75–109.

Fadyl, J., & Nicholls, D. (2013). Foucault, the subject and the research interview: A critique of methods. *Nursing Inquiry, 20* (1), 23–29.

Fairclough, N. (2013). Critical discourse analysis and critical policy studies. *Critical Policy Studies, 7*, 177–197.

Feldman, G. (2007). Following or facing the governmental gaze: Academic and policy intellectuals in the early twenty-first century, Roundtable, Conference of the Canadian Anthropological Society—American Ethnological Society, University of Toronto, May 8–12.

Fenna, A. (2004). *Australian public policy*, 2nd edition. Frenchs Forest: Pearson Education Australia.

Fernandez, B. (2012). *Transformative policy for poor women: A new feminist framework.* Surrey: Ashgate.

Finlayson, A., & Martin, J. (2006). Poststructructuralism. In C. Hay, M. Lister, D. Marsh (Eds.), *The state, theories and issues.* Basingstoke: Palgrave.
Fischer, F. (1980). *Politics, values and public policy: The problem of methodology.* Boulder, CO: Westview Press.
Fischer, F. (2003). *Reframing public policy: Discursive politics and deliberative practices.* Oxford: Oxford University Press.
Flynn, T. (1989). Symposiums papers: Foucault and the politics of postmodernity. *Noûs, 23* (2), 187–198.
Flynn, T. (2006). Foucault's mapping of history. In G. Gutting (Ed.), *The Cambridge companion to Foucault*, 2nd edition. Cambridge: Cambridge University Press.
Fontana, A., & Frey, J. (2005). The interview: From neutral stance to political involvement. In N. Denzin, & Y. Lincoln (Eds.), *The Sage Handbook of qualitative research*, 3rd edition, Thousand Oaks, USA: Sage.
Foucault, M. (1969). Pamphlet submitted to Professors of the Collège de France. Cited in D. Eribon (1991) *Michel Foucault*, Wing, B. (trans.). Cambridge, MA: Harvard University Press.
Foucault, M. (1972). *The archaeology of knowledge, and the discourse on language* (trans: Sheridan Smith, A.M.). New York: Pantheon Books.
Foucault, M. (1977) [1971]. Nietzsche, genealogy, history. In D.F. Bouchard, (Ed.), *Language, counter-memory, practice: Selected essays and interviews.* Ithaca: Cornell University Press.
Foucault, M. (1978). 1 May 1978. In G. Burchell (Trans.), *Michel Foucault: Security, territory, population, Lectures at the Collège de France, 1977–78.* South Yarra: Palgrave Macmillan.
Foucault, M. (1979). *Discipline and punish: The birth of the prison* (trans: Sheridan, A.). New York: Vintage/Random House.
Foucault, M. (1980). Two lectures. In C. Gordon (Ed.), *Michel Foucault power/ knowledge: Selected interviews and other writings 1972–1977 by Michel Foucault.* Gordon, C., Marshall, L., Mepham, J. and Soper, K. (trans.). New York: Pantheon Books.
Foucault, M. (1982). The subject and power. In H. Dreyfus, & P. Rabinow (Eds.), *Michel Foucault: Beyond structuralism and hermeneutics.* Chicago: University of Chicago Press.
Foucault, M. (1984a). The means of correct training [from *Discipline and Punish*]. In P. Rabinow (Ed.), *The Foucault reader.* New York: Pantheon Books.
Foucault, M. (1984b), What is Enlightenment? In P. Rabinow (Ed.), *The Foucault reader.* New York: Pantheon Books.
Foucault, M. (1986) [1984], *The use of pleasure. The history of sexuality, Volume 2,* (trans: Hurley, R.). London: Viking Press.
Foucault, M. (1987). The ethic of care for the self as a practice of freedom: An interview with Michel Foucault on January 20, 1984, with R. Fornet-

Betancourt, H. Becker, A. Gomez-Müller, J.C. Gauthier, *Philosophy & Social Criticism, 12*, 112–131.

Foucault, M. (1990a) [1978]. *The history of sexuality. Volume I: An introduction* (trans: Hurley, R.). New York: Vintage Books.

Foucault, M. (1990b). Critical theory/intellectual history. In L. Kritzman (Ed.), *Michel Foucault: Politics, philosophy, culture: Interviews & other writings 1977–1984*, 1st edition 1988, Sheridan, A. (trans.). London: Routledge.

Foucault, M. (1990c). The concern for truth. In L.D. Kritzman (Ed.), *Michel Foucault: Politics, philosophy, culture. Interviews and other writings, 1977–1984*, 1st edition 1988, A. Sheridan, (trans.). New York: Routledge.

Foucault, M. (1991a) [1978]. Politics and the study of discourse. In G. Burchell, C. Gordon, P. Miller (Eds.), *The Foucault effect: Studies in governmentality*. Chicago: University of Chicago Press.

Foucault, M. (1991b) [1981]. Questions of method. In G. Burchell, C. Gordon, P. Miller (Eds.), *The Foucault effect: Studies in governmentality*. Chicago: University of Chicago Press.

Foucault, M. (1991c) [1978]. Governmentality. In G. Burchell, C. Gordon, P. Miller (Eds.), *The Foucault effect: Studies in governmentality*. Chicago: University of Chicago Press.

Foucault, M. (1994a) [1981]. So is it important to think? In J.D. Faubion, (Ed.), *Power: Essential works of Foucault 1954–1984*, vol. 3, Hurley, R. and others (trans.). London: Penguin.

Foucault, M. (1994b). Table ronde du 20 mai 1978. In D. Defert, & F. Ewald (Eds.), *Michel Foucault: Dits et Écrits*, tome IV. Paris: Gallimard.

Foucault, M. (2000) [1982]. The subject and power. In J.D. Faubion (Ed.), *Power: Essential works of Foucault 1954–1984*, vol. 3, Hurley, R. and others (trans.). New York: The New Press.

Foucault, M. (2001) [1984]. *À propos de la généalogie de l'éthique: Un aperçu du travail en cours* (rewritten version). In D. Defert, & F. Ewald (Eds.), *Michel Foucault: Dits et Écrits*, tome II. Paris: Gallimard.

Foucault, M. (2003). Society must be defended. In M. Bertani, & A. Fontana (Eds.), *Lectures at the Collège de France, 1975–76*, Macey, D. (trans.). New York: Picador.

Foucault, M. (2008). The birth of biopolitics. In M. Senellart (Ed.), *Lectures at the Collège de France 1978–1979*, G. Burchell (trans.). New York: Palgrave Macmillan.

Foucault, M. (2009). *Security, territory, population: Lectures at the Collège de France 1977–1978*, Senellart, M. (ed.), Burchell, G. (trans.). Basingstoke: Palgrave Macmillan.

Fraser, S. (2013). Junk: Overeating and obesity and the neuroscience of addiction. *Addiction Research and Theory, 21* (6), 496–506.

Fraser, S., & Moore, D. (2011). Governing through problems: The formulation of policy on amphetamine-type stimulants (ATS) in Australia. *International Journal of Drug Policy*, *22*, 498–506.

Fraser, S., Moore, D., Keane, H. (2014). *Habits: Remaking addiction*. Houndmills: Palgrave Macmillan.

Freeman, R. (2006). The work the document does: Research, policy, and equity in health. *Journal of Health Politics, Policy and Law*, *31* (1), 51–70.

Fulcher, G. (1989). *Disabling policies? A comparative approach to education policy and disability*. East Sussex: The Falmer Press.

Gherardi, S. (2009). Introduction: The critical power of the "practice lens". *Management Learning*, *40* (2), 115–128.

Gibson, C., Dufty R., Phillips, S., Smith, H. (2008). Counter-geographies: The campaign against rationalisation of agricultural research stations in New South Wales. *Australian Journal of Rural Studies*, *24* (3), 351–366.

Gill, Z. (2012). Located subjects: The daily lives of policy workers. In A. Bletsas, & C. Beasley (Eds.), *Engaging with Carol Bacchi: Strategic interventions and exchanges*. Adelaide: University of Adelaide Press.

Glynos, J., & Howarth, D. (2007). *Logics of critical explanation in social and political theory*. London: Routledge.

Golder, B. (2010). Foucault and the unfinished human of rights. *Law, Culture and the Humanities*, *6* (3), 354–374.

Goodwin, N. (1996). Governmentality in the Queensland Department of Education: Policies and the management of schools. *Discourse: Studies in the Cultural Politics of Education*, *17* (1), 65–74.

Goodwin, S. (2011). Analysing policy as discourse: Methodological advances in policy analysis. In L. Markauskaite, P. Freebody, J. Irwin (Eds.), *Methodological choice and design: Scholarship, policy and practice in social and educational research*. London, New York: Springer, Dordrecht, Heidelberg.

Goodwin, S., & Voola, A. (2013). Framing microfinance in Australia – gender neutral or gender blind? *Australian Journal of Social Issues*, *48* (2), 223–239.

Gordon, C. (1991). Governmental rationality: An introduction. In G. Burchell, C. Gordon, P. Miller (Eds.), *The Foucault effect: Studies in governmentality*. Chicago: University of Chicago Press.

Government of South Australia (2012). *Primary industries and regions South Australia (PIRSA) Strategic Directions 2012–2015*. Adelaide: Government of South Australia.

Grebe, C. (2009). *Reconciliation policy in Germany 1998–2008: Construing the "problem" of the incompatibility of paid employment and care work*, PhD Dissertation, University of Nottingham, VS Verlag für Sozialwissenschaften, Weisbaden.

Green, K., Tones, K., Cross, R., Woodall, J. (2015). *Health promotion: Planning and strategies*. London: Sage.

Gugerli, D. (1998). Politics on the topographer's table: The Helvetic triangulation of cartography, politics, and representation. In T. Lenoir (Ed.), *Inscribing science: Scientific texts and the materiality of communication.* California: Stanford University Press.

Gulson, K.N., & Metcalfe, A.S. (2015). Introduction: Education policy analysis for a complex world: Poststructural possibilities. *Critical Studies in Education, 56* (1), 1–4.

Gusfield, J. (1996). *Contested meanings: The construction of alcohol problems.* Madison: University of Wisconsin Press.

Hacking, I. (1986). Making up people. In T. Heller, & C. Brooke-Rose, (Eds.), *Reconstructing individualism: Autonomy, individuality and the self in Western thought.* Stanford, California: Stanford University Press.

Hanna, P., Johnson, S., Stenner, P., Adams, M. (2015). Foucault, sustainable tourism, and relationships with the environment (human and nonhuman). *GeoJournal, 80* (2), 301–314.

Hansen, M.P. (2014). Non-normative critique: Foucault and pragmatic sociology as tactical re-politicization. *European Journal of Social Theory* [online], 21 December, doi: 10.1177/1368431014562705.

Harris, P. (1999). Public welfare and liberal governance. In A. Petersen, I. Barns, J. Dudley, P. Harris (Eds.), *Poststructuralism, citizenship and social policy.* London: Routledge.

Haugaard, M., & Clegg, S. (2009). Introduction: Why power is the central concept of the social sciences. In S. Clegg, & M. Haugaard (Eds.), *The Sage handbook of power.* London: Sage.

Haydock, W. (2014). The rise and fall of the "nudge" of minimum unit pricing: The continuity of neoliberalism in alcohol policy in England. *Critical Social Policy, 34*, 260–279.

Hearn, J., & McKie, L. (2010). Gendered and social hierarchies in problem representation and policy processes: "Domestic violence" in Finland and Scotland, *Violence Against Women, 16* (2), 136–158.

Henderson, J., & Fuller, J. (2011). "Problematising" Australian policy representations in responses to the physical health of people with mental health disorders. *Australian Journal of Social Issues, 46* (2), 183–203.

Henman, P. (2006). Segmentation and conditionality: Technological reconfigurations in social policy and social citizenship. In G. Marston, & C. McDonald, (Eds.), *Analysing social policy: A governmental approach.* Cheltenham: Edward Elgar.

Hindess, B. (2000). Citizenship in the international management of populations. *American Behavioral Scientist, 43* (9), 1486–1497.

Hoagland, S.L. (1988). *Lesbian ethics: Toward new value.* Palo Alto, CA: Institute of Lesbian Studies.

Hoffman, J., & Graham, P. (2006). *Introduction to political concepts.* Essex: Pearson Education.

Holmgren, S. (2015). *Governing forests in a changing climate: Exploring patterns of thought at the climate change-forest policy intersection*, PhD Thesis, Swedish University of Agricultural Sciences, Uppsala.

Holmgren, S., & Arora-Jonsson, S. (2015). The Forest Kingdom – with what values for the world? Climate change and gender equality in a contested forest policy context, *Scandinavian Journal of Forest Research*, *30* (3), 235–245.

Holstein, J., & Gubrium, J. (eds) (2003). *Inside interviewing: New lenses, new concerns*. Thousand Oaks: Sage.

Holstein, J., & Gubrium, J. (2011). The constructionist analytics of interpretive practice. In N. Denzin, & Y. Lincoln (Eds.), *The Sage handbook of qualitative research*, 4th edition. Thousand Oaks: Sage.

Hoppe, R. (2002). Cultures of public policy problems. *Journal of Comparative Policy Analysis: Research and Practice*, *4* (3), 305–326.

Hoppe, R. (2011). *The governance of problems: Puzzling, power and participation*. Bristol: Polity Press.

Hudson, C. (2012). New subject positions for non-traditional actors or business as usual in the strong region discourse. In S. Anderson, K. Berglund, E. Gunnarsson, E. Sundin, (Eds.), *Promoting innovation: Policies, practices and procedures*, VINNOVA Report VR 2012.08, Swedish Governmental Agency for Innovation System, Stockholm.

Inda, J. (2005). Analytics of the modern: An introduction. In J. Inda (Ed.), *Anthropologies of modernity: Foucault, governmentality and life politics*. Malden: Blackwell.

Jann, W., & Wegrich, K. (2007). Theories of the policy cycle. In F. Fischer, G.J. Miller, M.S. Sidney (Eds.), *Handbook of public policy analysis: Theory, politics, and methods*. Boca Raton, Florida: CRC Press.

John, P. (1998). *Analyzing Public Policy*. London: Routledge.

Johnson, B. (1981). Translator's introduction. In J. Derrida, *Dissemination*, B. Johnson (trans.) Chicago: University of Chicago Press.

Jones, A. (1997). Teaching post-structuralist feminist theory in education: Student resistances. *Gender and Education*, *9* (3), 261–269.

Jørgensen, M.B. (2012). Legitimizing policies: How policy approaches to irregular migrants are formulated and legitimized in Scandinavia. *Nordic Journal of Applied Ethics*, *6* (2), 46–53.

Keane, H., Moore, D., Fraser, S. (2011). Addiction and dependence: Making realities in the *DSM*. *Addiction*, *106*, 875–877.

Kelly, S.J. (2015). *Governing civil society: How literacy, education and security were brought together*, PhD thesis, Faculty of Education, Queensland University of Technology.

Kingdon, J.W. (2003). *Agendas, alternatives, and public policies*, 1st edition 1984. New York: Longman.

Kok, M., & de Coninck, H. (2007). Widening the scope of politics to address climate change: Directions for mainstreaming. *Environment Science & Policy, 10* (7–8), 587–599.

Koopman, C. (2013). *Genealogy as critique: Foucault and the problems of modernity*. Bloomington: Indiana University Press.

Kuehls, T. (1996). *Beyond sovereign territory: The space of ecopolitics*. Minneapolis: University of Minnesota Press.

Kulynych, J.J. (1997). Performing politics: Foucault, Habermas and postmodern participation. *Polity, 30* (2), 315–346.

Kvist, E., & Peterson, E. (2010). What has gender equality got to do with it? An analysis of policy debates surrounding domestic services in the welfare states of Spain and Sweden. *NORA—Nordic Journal of Feminist and Gender Research, 18* (3), 185–203.

Lake, M. (2006). From Mississippi to Melbourne via Natal: The invention of the literacy test as a technology of racial exclusion. In A. Curthoys, & M. Lake (Eds.), *Connected worlds: History in transnational perspective*. Canberra: ANU Press.

Lakoff, G. (1987). *Women, fire, and dangerous things: What categories reveal about the mind*. Chicago: University of Chicago Press.

Lall, M. (2007). *A review of concepts from policy studies relevant for the analysis of EFA [Education for All] in developing countries*, Consortium for Research on Educational Access, Transitions & Equity (CREATE), Sussex.

Lall, M. (ed.) (2012). *Policy, discourse and rhetoric: How New Labour challenged social justice and democracy*. Rotterdam: Sense Publishers.

Lancaster, K. (2014). Social construction and the evidence-based drug policy endeavour. *International Journal of Drug Policy, 25*, 948–951.

Lancaster, K., Duke, K., Ritter, A. (2015). Producing the "problem of drugs": A cross-national comparison of "recovery" discourse in two Australian and British reports. *International Journal of Drug Policy, 26*, 617–625.

Lancaster, K., Hughes, C.E., Chalmers, J., Ritter, A. (2012). More than problem-solving: Critical reflections on the "problematisation" of alcohol-related violence in Kings Cross. *Drug and Alcohol Review, 31*, 925–927.

Lancaster, K., Ritter, A., Colebatch, H. (2014). Problems, policy and politics: Making sense of Australia's "ice epidemic". *Policy Studies, 35* (2), 147–171.

Lancaster, K., Seear, K., Treloar, C. (2015). Laws prohibiting peer distribution of injecting equipment in Australia: A critical analysis of their effects. *International Journal of Drug Policy, 16* (12), 1198–1206.

Larner, W. (2000). Neo-liberalism: Policy, ideology, governmentality. *Studies in Political Economy, 63*, 5–25.

Larner, W. (2008). Comments on Kevin Stenson's "Governing the local: Sovereignty, social governance and community safety". *Social Work and Society – International Online Journal*, *6* (1), 21–25, www.socwork.net/sws/article/download/87/144. Accessed 14 January, 2016.

Larner, W., & Walters, W. (2004). Introduction: Global governmentality. In W. Larner, & W. Walters (Eds.), *Global governmentality: Governing international spaces*. New York: Routledge.

Lasswell, H.D. (1956). *The decision process: Seven categories of functional analysis*. College Park: University of Maryland Press.

Laurier, E., & Philo, C. (2004). Ethnoarchaeology and undefined investigations. *Environment and Planning A*, *36*, 421–436.

Law, J. (2004). *After method: Mess in social science research*. London and New York: Routledge.

Levine, H.G. (1984). The alcohol problem in America: From temperance to alcoholism. *British Journal of Addiction*, *79*, 109–118.

Lindblom, C.E. (1980). *The policy-making process*, 2nd edition. Englewood Cliffs, NJ: Prentice-Hall.

Lister, R. (2010). *Understanding theories and concepts in social policy*. Bristol: Policy Press.

Logan, H., Sumsion, J., Press, C. (2013). The Child Care Act 1972: A critical juncture in Australian ECEC and the emergence of "quality". *Australian Journal of Early Childhood*, *38* (4), 84–91.

MacLeod, G., & Jones, M. (2011). Re*newing* urban politics. *Urban Studies*, *48* (12), 2443–2472.

Maddison, S., & Denniss, N. (2013). *An introduction to Australian public policy: Theory and practice*, 2nd edition. Melbourne: Cambridge University Press.

Manning, S. (2014). Parents, policy and playcentre: Developing a critical research proposal. In J. Rath, & C. Mutch (Eds.), *Emerging critical scholarship in education: Navigating the doctoral journey*. Newcastle upon Tyne: Cambridge Scholars Publishing.

Marginson, S. (1997). Subjects and subjugation: The economics of education as power-knowledge. *Discourse: Studies in the Cultural Politics of Education*, *18* (2), 215–227.

Marsh, I. (2013). The uses of history in the unmaking of modern suicide. *Journal of Social History*, *46* (3), 744–756.

Marshall, N. (2012a). *Disability, inclusive development and the World Bank: The construction and problematisation of disability in international development policy*, PhD thesis, Faculty of Social Sciences and Law, University of Bristol.

Marshall, N. (2012b). Digging deeper: The challenge of problematising "inclusive development" and "disability mainstreaming". In A. Bletsas, & C. Beasley (Eds.), *Engaging with Carol Bacchi: Strategic interventions and exchanges*. Adelaide: University of Adelaide Press.

Martin, F., & Aston, S. (2014). A "special population" with "unique treatment needs": Dominant representations of "women's substance abuse" and their effects. *Contemporary Drug Problems*, *41*, 355–360.

Massey, D. (1994). *Space, place and gender*. Minneapolis: University of Minnesota Press.

Massey, D. (2005). *For space*. London: Sage.

Mausethagen, S. (2013). Governance through concepts: The OECD and the construction of "competence" in Norwegian education policy. *Berkeley Review of Education*, *4* (1), 161–181.

McDowell, M.G., & Wonders, N.A. (2009–2010). Keeping migrants in their place: Technologies of control and racialized public space in Arizona. *Social Justice*, *36* (2), 54–72.

McEwan, C., & Butler, R. (2007). Disability and development: Different models, different places. *Geography Compass*, *1* (3), 448–466.

McHoul, A., & Grace, W. (1993). *A Foucault primer: Discourse, power and the subject*. Melbourne: Melbourne University Press.

McLeod, J., & Wright, K. (2015). Inventing youth wellbeing. In K. Wright, & J. McLeod (Eds.), *Rethinking youth wellbeing: Critical perspectives*. Singapore: Springer.

McPhee, H. (2001). A course to nowhere. *The Melbourne Age*, 4 August.

Middendorp, C. (2002). Homelessness and public space: Unwelcome visitors. *Parity*, *15* (1), 18.

Miller, P. (2001). Governing by numbers: Why calculative practices matter. *Social Research*, *68* (2), 379–396.

Miller, P., & Rose, N. (1990). Governing economic life. *Economy and Society*, *19* (1), 1–31.

Ministry of Education and Research (2004). *Kultur for læring* [*Culture for learning*] (White Paper 30 [2003–2004]), The Ministry, Oslo, Norway.

Mitchell, K. (2006). Neoliberal governmentality in the European Union: Education, training and technologies of citizenship. *Environment and Planning D: Society and Space*, *24*, 389–407.

Mohanty, C.T. (1991). Under western eyes: Feminist scholarship and colonial discourses. In C.T. Mohanty, A. Russo, L. Torres (Eds.), *Third world women and the politics of feminism*. Bloomington: Indiana University Press.

Moisander, J., Valtonen, A., Hirsto, H. (2009). Personal interviews in cultural consumer research – post-structuralist challenges. *Consumption Markets and Culture*, *12* (4), 329–348.

Mol, A. (1999). Ontological politics: A word and some questions. In J. Law, & J. Hassard (Eds.), *Actor network theory and after*. Oxford: Blackwell.

Mol, A. (2002). *The body multiple: Ontology in medical practice*. Durham and London: Duke University Press.

Moore, D., & Fraser, S. (2013). Producing the "problem" of addiction in drug treatment. *Qualitative Health Research*, *23* (7), 916–923.

Moss, J. (1998). Introduction: The later Foucault. In J. Moss (Ed.), *The later Foucault: Politics and philosophy*. London: Sage.

Mouffe, C. (2005). *On the political.* London and New York: Verso.

New South Wales Department of Health (2009). *Physical health care of mental health consumers: Guidelines.* North Sydney: NSW Department of Health.

Nielsen, R., & Bonham, J. (2015). More than a message: Producing cyclists through public safety advertising campaigns. In J. Bonham, & M. Johnson (Eds.), *Cycling futures.* Adelaide: University of Adelaide Press.

Northern Territory of Australia (2014). *Northern Territory Second Reading Speeches, Police Administration Amendment Bill 2014*, http://www.austlii.edu.au/au/legis/nt/bill_srs/paab2014317/srs.html. Accessed 2 January 2016.

OECD (2013). *How's life? 2013: Measuring well-being.* Paris: OECD Publishing.

O'Malley, P., Weir, L., Shearing, C. (1997). Governmentality, criticism, politics. *Economy and Society*, *26* (4), 501–517.

Osborne, T. (1997). Of health and statecraft. In A. Petersen, & R. Bunton (Eds.), *Foucault: Health and medicine.* London: Routledge.

Papatsiba, V. (2014). Policy goals of European integration and competitiveness in academic collaborations: An examination of Joint Master's and Erasmus Mundus Programmes. *Higher Education Policy*, *27* (1), 43–64.

Partridge, E. (2014). *Words and silences: The discursive politics of problem representation in the Northern Territory Intervention*, PhD thesis, University of New South Wales, Sydney.

Pawson, R., & Tilley, N. (2004). *Realist evaluation*, funded by British Cabinet Office, www.communitymatters.com.au/RE_chapter.pdf. Accessed 31 December 2015.

Payne, S. (2014). Constructing the gendered body? A critical discourse analysis of gender equality schemes in the health sector in England. *Current Sociology*, *62* (7), 956–974.

Pease, B. (2011). Governing men's violence against women in Australia. In E. Ruspini, J. Hearn, B. Pease, K. Pringle, (Eds.), *Men and masculinities around the world: Transforming men's practices.* New York: Palgrave Macmillan.

Pereira, R.B. (2014). Using critical policy analysis in occupational science research: Exploring Bacchi's methodology. *Journal of Occupational Science*, *21* (4), 389–402.

Postill, J. (2010). Introduction: Theorizing media and practice. In B. Bräuchler, & J. Postill (Eds.), *Theorizing media and practice.* Oxford and New York: Berghahn.

Poulson, H. (2006). *The elusive gender: the International Labour Organization and the construction of gender equality*, PhD Thesis, Department of Political Science, University of Copenhagen.

Powell, A., & Murray, S. (2008). Children and domestic violence: Constructing a policy problem in Australia and New Zealand. *Social & Legal Studies*, *17* (4), 453–473.

Pringle, R., & Watson, S. (1992). "Women's interests" and the post-structuralist state. In M. Barrett, & A. Phillips (Eds.), *Destabilizing theory: Contemporary feminist debates.* California: Stanford University Press.

Prügl, E. (2015). Neoliberalising feminism. *New Political Economy, 20* (4), 614–631, doi:10.1080/13563467.2014.951614.

Rabinow, P. (2003). *Anthropos today: Reflections on modern equipment.* Princeton: Princeton University Press.

Race, K. (2005). Recreational states: Drugs and the sovereignty of consumption. *Culture Machine*, 7, 1–10.

Razack, S. (2002). *Race, space, and the law: Unmapping a white settler society.* Toronto: Between the Lines Press.

Rein, M., & Schön, D. (1977). Problem setting in policy research. In C. Weiss (Ed.), *Using research in public policy making.* Lexington, MA: Lexington Books.

Ristovski-Slijepcevic, S., Chapman, G., Beagan, B. (2010). Being a "good mother": Dietary governmentality in the family food practices of three ethnocultural groups in Canada. *Health, 14* (5), 467–483.

Rönnblom, M. (2012). Post-structural comparative politics: Acknowledging the political effects of research. In A. Bletsas, & C. Beasley (Eds.), *Engaging with Carol Bacchi: Strategic interventions and exchanges.* Adelaide: University of Adelaide Press.

Rönnblom, M., & Keisu, B. (2013). Constructions of innovation and gender (equality) in Swedish universities. *International Journal of Gender & Entrepreneurship, 5* (3), 342–356.

Rönnblom, M., & Sandberg, L. (2015). Imagining the ideal city, planning the gender-equal city, Paper presented at the RC21 International Conference on "The Ideal City: between myth and reality", Urbino (Italy), 27–29 August, http://www.rc21.org/en/conferences/urbino2015/. Accessed 20 November 2014.

Room, R. (1983). Sociological aspects of the disease concept of alcoholism. In R. Smart (Ed.), *Research advances in alcohol and drug problems.* New York and London: Plenum Press.

Rose, N. (1991). Governing by numbers: Figuring out democracy. *Accounting, Organizations and Society, 16* (7), 673–692.

Rose, N. (2000). *Powers of freedom: Reframing political thought*, 1st edition 1999. Cambridge: Cambridge University Press.

Rose, N., & Miller, P. (1992). Political power beyond the state: Problematics of government. *The British Journal of Sociology, 43* (2), 173–205.

Rose, N., O'Malley, P., Valverde, M. (2006). Governmentality, *Annual Review of Law and Social Science, 2*, 83–104.

Rosenberg, C.F. (2003). What is disease? In memory of Owsei Temkin. *Bulletin of the History of Medicine, 77* (3), 491–505.

Rowse, T. (2009). The ontological politics of "closing the gaps". *Journal of Cultural Economy, 2* (1&2), 33–48.

Salter, P. (2013). The problem in policy: Representations of Asia literacy in Australian education for the Asian century. *Asian Studies Review*, *37* (1), 3–20.

Sandberg, L., & Rönnblom, M. (2014). "I don't think we'll ever be finished with this": Fear and safety in policy and practice. *Urban Studies*, 1–16. DOI: 10.1177/0042098014550453.

Sanger, T. (2008). Trans governmentality: The production and regulation of gendered subjectivities. *Journal of Gender Studies*, *17* (1), 41–53.

Sawicki, J. (1991). *Disciplining Foucault: Feminism, power, and the body*. New York and London: Routledge.

Schatzki, T. (2001). Introduction: Practice theory. In T. Schatzki, K.K. Cetina, E. von Savigny (Eds.), *The practice turn in contemporary theory*. London and New York: Routledge.

Schön, D.A. (1979). Generative metaphor: A perspective on problem-setting in social policy. In A. Ortony (Ed.), *Metaphor and thought*. Cambridge: Cambridge University Press.

Seear, K., & Fraser, S. (2014). The addict as victim: Producing the "problem" of addiction in Australian victims of crime compensation laws. *International Journal of Drug Policy*, *25*, 826–835.

Shapiro, I. (2002). Problems, methods, and theories in the study of politics, or what's wrong with political science and what to do about it. *Political Theory*, *30*, 596–619.

Shapiro, M.J. (1992). *Reading the postmodern polity: Political theory as textual practice*. Minneapolis: University of Minnesota Press.

Shaw, S.E. (2010). Reaching the parts that other theories and methods can't reach: How and why a policy-as-discourse approach can inform health-related policy. *Health*, *14* (2), 196–212.

Shore, C. (2012). Anthropology and public policy. In R. Fardon, T. Harris, T.H.J. Marchand, C. Shore, V. Strang, R. Wilson, M. Nuttall (Eds.), *The Sage handbook of Social Anthropology*. London: Sage.

Shore, C., & Wright, S. (2003). Policy: A new field of Anthropology. In C. Shore, & S. Wright (Eds.), *Anthropology of policy: Perspectives on governance and power*. New York: Routledge.

Shore, C., & Wright, S. (2011). Conceptualising policy: Technologies of governance and the politics of visibility. In C. Shore, S. Wright, D. Però (Eds.), *Policy worlds: Anthropology and the analysis of contemporary power*. New York: Berghahn Books.

Simon, H. (1961) [1945]. *Administrative behavior: A study of decision-making processes in administrative organization*, 2nd edition. New York: Macmillan.

Smart, C. (1996). Deconstructing motherhood. In E. Silva (Ed.), *Good enough mothering? Feminist perspectives on lone motherhood*. London: Routledge.

Smith, K.E., Hunter, D.J., Blackman, T., Elliot, E., Green, A., Harrington, B. E., Marks, L., McKee, L., Williams, G.H. (2009). Divergence or convergence?

Health inequalities and policy in a devolved Britain. *Critical Social Policy, 29* (2), 216–242.

Southgate, E., & Bennett, A. (2014). Excavating widening participation policy in Australian higher education: Subject positions, representational effects, emotion. *Creative Approaches to Research, 7* (1), 21–45.

St. Pierre, E.A. (2000). Poststructural feminism in education: An overview. *International Journal of Qualitative Studies in Education, 13* (5), 477–515.

St. Pierre, E.A. (2006). Scientifically based research in education: Epistemology and ethics. *Adult Education Quarterly, 56*, 239–266.

St. Pierre, E. (2011). Post qualitative research: The critique and the coming after. In N.K. Denzin, & Y.S. Lincoln (Eds.), *The Sage handbook of qualitative research*, 4th edition. Thousand Oaks: Sage.

Stern, M. (2006). Racism, sexism, classism, and much more: Reading security-identity in marginalized sites. In B. Ackerly, M. Stern, J. True (Eds.), *Feminist methodologies for international relations*. Cambridge: Cambridge University Press.

Sutton, C. (1998). *Swedish alcohol discourse: Constructions of a social problem* (Dissertation for the Degree of Doctor of Philosophy & Sociology), Uppsala, Sweden: *Acta Universitatis Upsaliensis. Studia Sociologica Upsaliensia*, 45.

Sutton, R. (1999). *The policy process: An overview*. London: Overseas Development Institute.

Tamboukou, M. (1999). Writing genealogies: An exploration of Foucault's strategies for doing research. *Discourse: Studies in the Cultural Politics of Education, 20* (2), 201–217.

Tanesini, A. (1994). Whose language? In K. Lennon, & M. Whitford (Eds.), *Knowing the difference: Feminist perspectives in epistemology*. New York: Routledge.

Tietäväinen, A., Pyykkönene, M., Kaisto, J. (2008). Globalization and power – governmentalization of Europe? An interview with William Walters. *Foucault Studies, 5*, 63–73.

Tilley, N. (2010). Whither problem-oriented policing? *Criminology and Public Policy, 9* (1), 183–195.

Turnbull, N. (2005). *Policy in question: From problem solving to problematology*, PhD thesis, School of Social Science and Policy, University of New South Wales, Sydney.

UKDPC (2008). *The UK Drug Policy Commission Recovery Consensus Group: A vision of recovery*. London: UK Drug Policy Commission.

UNHCR (United Nations High Commissioner for Refugees) (2015). Worldwide displacement hits all-time high as war and persecution increase. *News Stories*, 18 June, http://www.unhcr.org/558193896.html. Accessed 20 November 2015.

UNICEF (2013). *Child well-being in rich countries: A comparative overview* (Innocenti Report Card 11). Florence: UNICEF Office of Research.

Valverde, M. (1998). *Diseases of the will: Alcohol and the dilemmas of freedom.* Cambridge: Cambridge University Press.

van Houtum, H. (2005). The geopolitics of borders and boundaries. *Geopolitics, 10*, 672–679.

Vasagar, J. (2012). Privately owned public space: Where are they and who owns them? *The Guardian*, London.

Veyne, P. (1997). Foucault revolutionizes history. In A.I. Davidson (Ed.), *Foucault and his Interlocutors*, Porter, C. (trans.), Chicago: University of Chicago Press.

VLRC (Victorian Law Reform Commission) (2010). *Surveillance in public places, Final Report 18.* Melbourne: Victorian Law Reform Commission.

Wade, M. (2015). Key measure of Australia's wellbeing has been stagnant for two years. *The Age*, September 5.

Walker, R.B.J. (1993). *Inside/outside: International relations as political theory.* Cambridge: Cambridge University Press.

Walters, W. (2002a). The power of inscription: Beyond social construction and deconstruction in European integration studies. *Millennium: Journal of International Studies, 31* (3), 83–108.

Walters, W. (2002b). Mapping Schengenland: Denaturalizing the border. *Environment and Planning D: Society and Space, 20*, 561–580.

Walters, W. (2004). Secure borders, safe haven, domopolitics. *Citizenship Studies, 8*, 237–260.

Walters, W. (2006). "The end of the passing past": Towards polytemporal policy studies. In G. Marston, & C. McDonald (Eds.), *Reframing social policy: A governmental approach.* London: Edward Elgar.

Walters, W. (2009). Europe's borders. In C. Rumford (Ed.), *The Sage handbook of European Studies.* London: Sage.

Watson, S. (2000). Foucault and the study of social policy. In G. Lewis, S. Gerwitz, J. Clarke (Eds.), *Rethinking social policy.* New York: Open University Press.

Webb, P.T. (2014). Policy problematization. *International Journal of Qualitative Studies in Education, 27* (3), 364–376.

Weedon, C. (1987). *Feminist practice and poststructuralist theory.* Oxford, UK: Basil Blackwell.

WHO (World Health Organization) (1980). *Expert Committee Report on Problems Related to Alcohol Consumption* (WHO Technical Report Series 650), World Health Organization, Geneva.

WHO (World Health Organization) (2010). *Global strategy on the harmful use of alcohol.* Geneva: WHO.

WHO (World Health Organization) (2015). *Health in all policies: Training manual.* Geneva: World Health Organization.

Widding, U. (2011). Problematic parents and the community parent education: Representations of social class, ethnicity, and gender. *Journal of Feminist Family Therapy, 23* (1), 19–38.

Wildavsky, A. (1979). *The art and craft of policy analysis.* London: Macmillan.

Wilson, D., Rose, J., Colvin, E. (2010). *Marginalised young people, surveillance & public space: A research report.* Melbourne: Youth Affairs Council of Victoria and the School of Political and Social Inquiry, Monash University.

Wiseman, N. (2012). *"Food" for thought: A post-structural analysis of "food" and the implications for agriculture in urban and peri-urban regions*, Masters of Planning Dissertation, Geography, Environment and Population, School of Social Sciences, University of Adelaide.

Wright, K., & McLeod, J. (eds) (2015). *Rethinking youth wellbeing: Critical perspectives.* Singapore: Springer.

Zournazi, M. (2002). Navigating movements: An interview with Brian Massumi. In M. Zournazi (Ed.), *Hope: New Philosophies for Change.* Annandale, NSW: Pluto Press.

Zufferey, C. (2014). Questioning representations of homelessness in the Australian print media. *Australian Social Work, 67* (4), 525–536.

Index

C. Bacchi, S. Goodwin, *Poststructural Policy Analysis*,
DOI 10.1057/978-1-137-52546-8

Lightning Source UK Ltd.
Milton Keynes UK
UKHW020137031121
393274UK00003B/215

9 781137 525444